Molly II
Am I Who I Should Be?

by

Rosemarie Smith

www.littlemolly.co.uk

**Grosvenor House
Publishing Limited**

This book is published by
Grosvenor House Publishing Ltd
28-30 High Street, Guildford, Surrey, GU1 3HY.
www.grosvenorhousepublishing.co.uk

A CIP record for this book
is available from the British Library

ISBN 978-1-907652-34-9

In Molly II, I have tried to give some insight into the aftermath that occurs in a victim's life following child abuse. It is a true account of my broken marriages, failed relationships, abduction and attempted murder.

Rosemarie Smith

This book is dedicated to all those who have struggled through life as I have. To all who have suffered abuse and neglect and to those who are still suffering.

God bless you all

Foreword

Am I who I should be..? This is a question that I have always asked myself. I look back over my life and wonder how I ever survived the terrible trauma of sexual abuse and abandonment and the heartbreak of so many broken relationships, then I cast my mind back to the rare occasions when I felt safe and happy; then I thank God... I was one of the lucky ones.

I was aged fourteen when I first considered writing my autobiography, but then the reality of a broken home and abused childhood influenced my decision to postpone it until after the death of my parents, as I felt that their being made aware of the full devastation that occurred during their absence would have affected their psychological state far more than I would have wanted. Even now, years after their passing, I cannot find it within my heart to persecute them for something that I feel society helped to create.

When I first started writing 'Little Molly', I had no inclination whatsoever that it would result in my writing a sequel. Part two and part three of Little Molly both depict the true story of a young mother and her children's struggle to survive after being destroyed by the effects and aftermath of child abuse.

As a young woman I was under the illusion that my life had returned to normal and was pretty much like everyone else's, but then as I experienced first one unstable relationship after another, I realised that living in constant fear and suffering both physical and mental abuse was far from normal. This is the continuing story of my life as Little Molly. It is a true account of all the physical and mental suffering which my children and I incurred after the sexual abuse I suffered as a small child through to adulthood. It describes in explicit detail how I was kidnapped, and my assailant's attempt to murder me. It also includes my long, extended fight to regain custody of my three youngest children, Cheniel, Kyle and Allishia, following a breakdown and diagnosis of my epilepsy.

Author's Notes

Some of the names in this book have been changed in order to protect the innocent. As with 'Little Molly', I have decided to omit certain memories for the sake of my family. If, however, I have offended anyone, I apologise most sincerely.

This is an extract taken from my first book, 'Little Molly' by Rosemarie Smith

'I wasn't very old when I began to realise that no amount of hoping and wishing would ever change anything. If I wanted to survive the cold, cruel abuse and abandonment then I had to hide away my weaknesses and radiate strength. I hated the dark nights; they seemed to last forever. There were many times when I woke up crying during the night, wondering why I was so cold… Looking over my sleeping siblings I cried silently so as not to alarm them. I lived my life with poverty and hunger. If it had been just those two things maybe it wouldn't have been so bad but I hated the sexual abuse from my brother. I spent a lot of my childhood heartbroken and feeling miserable, desperately trying to get over everything that made me unhappy, wishing that I could grow up faster and praying for things to change. I made wishes that I would grow old and die before my time. All I wanted was the pain to stop.'

Ernest

Ernest is not an imaginary friend;
he is not a sound or a scene.

He's in every little girl's conscience;
he's a moment, a nightmare, a dream.

He cannot be described or forgotten,
he exists in any shape or form,

In a little girl's memory as a demon.
No date to which he was born.

He may appear all tongue-tied and twisted;
he may appear merry or forlorn.

He may appear and rest on one's shoulders,
in the evening, afternoon or dawn.

He is neither man, beast or structure,
of heights impossible to impose.

In every little girl's conscience, Ernest
preys where fear grows.

Perched on the slide in a play park,
on a swing or a sledge in the snow,

Why does he exist on such ruin? I would
beg him; take leave and let go.

But he who has no reason to comply for
he will gain no reward,

If only I could reason with Ernest, I would
have no fear at all.

Acknowledgement

Had it not been for the following people my story would not have been told.

My counsellor Clive Powell: I have so many things to thank you for it would take a whole book to list them all, many heartfelt thanks.

Many Thanks to Mike Powell from New Zealand for supplying the photograph of my beautiful daughter Cheniel for the front cover.

I would once again like to thank everyone at Grosvenor House Publishing For their speed when replying to my e-mails, for their patience when answering my questions and for their professionalism when piecing my second book together: many thanks to you all.

And finally to my children Ian, Cheniel, Kyle and Allishia who I want to thank from the bottom of my heart for being very patient and understanding. I know it has not been easy for you but still you have supported me. Thanks Kids you are an absolute treasure and I love you all.

Contents

CONTENTS

This is the continuation of my story 'Little Molly'

It is a true story of betrayal, heartbreak and misrepresentation

How am I supposed to write when my educational skills are so limited? I first asked myself this question when my counsellor, Clive Powell, challenged me into writing my first book 'Little Molly'. Now I want to go on and write about all the people who have had a significant effect on my life, it seems even more difficult. I know the kind of things I want to say about the people I have met, but there before my eyes appears that same blank screen that has haunted me all of my life. I suppose in a way the kind of life that I have had makes writing about it a little more difficult, yet I hear a voice inside my head that cries out for me to do it, so I know the right words will come to mind eventually.

Rosemarie Smith

✥ CHAPTER 1 ✥

A Small Part of my Life

When I cast my mind back to the poor example of a childhood that I had, the first person who comes to mind is Tyrone. He has been at the back of my mind for thirty-five years and, for reasons I don't understand, he has remained within my thoughts since the first day I met him. I was almost ten years old when we met. I had been placed at the Outrake Children's Home alongside my youngest sister, Lorraine, and my younger brother, Andrew, following the break-up of my family and our abandonment. I was totally devastated with the things that were going on around me and I was left severely traumatised. I seemed to blank situations that affected me personally and paid more attention to those who were kind to me.

One of my earliest memories takes me back to my first day at the Juniors School in the beautiful rural village of Ashford-in-the-Water in Derbyshire, where Tyrone was a pupil. It was strange really, in certain ways he reminded me so much of myself yet I could not bring myself to speak to him. He was abrupt and outspoken but I was shy and withdrawn. After suffering many years of abuse, I trusted no-one and found it almost impossible to make any exceptions. I was one out of many Outrake children who attended that school and at first seemed to be accepted more readily than I expected; the local children seemed to accept different faces as the norm and didn't question our sudden appearance, for which I was grateful. Having been removed from my family home by the local social services department, I had already spent a considerable amount of time living in a previous children's home at Duffield in Derby, so the last thing I needed was embarrassing questions. My first placement in the classroom at Ashford was a seat next to Tyrone. For some reason when the headmaster scanned the overcrowded classroom for a vacant chair for me to sit on, Tyrone jumped up with his hand raised high shouting, 'Please sir, please sir, there's a seat next to me!' Although Mr Parker hesitated for a while, after repeatedly glaring over at Tyrone then down at me, he allowed me to sit next to him. I remember pleading with Mr Parker beneath my breath, hoping he wouldn't allow me to sit next to such a distasteful looking character, but it was usual for me not to protest and I accepted the seat without question, although I hated the very thought of sitting next to a boy, especially one that was so untidy that he looked as though he had just been dragged through a hedge backwards. As I slumped down on the only available seat in the classroom, I hung my head in embarrassment and focused on Tyrone's dirty hands and soiled fingernails. Taking no particular notice of any other child in the room, I gradually viewed Tyrone from head to foot and considered him to be the most grubby child I had ever seen; taking apart myself and my younger siblings, of course, when we lived back home.

Having lived in care homes for some time, I was now viewing things from the other side of the fence, so to speak. I bathed each day and woke up to clean clothing, I owned a pair of leather shoes and wiped my nose on a clean white handkerchief, so I frowned upon the child who resembled a waif and stray. I too found it impossible to see the little boy underneath that grime and dirt and, because I had moved on, I was afraid to look any deeper, knowing there was a slight possibility of a child exactly like myself lurking underneath that rough exterior.

Ashford School was different to other schools I had attended; it was very small and compact. Despite it being situated in a rural district the teachers had a kind of mannerism which helped children like myself feel free to express themselves and show joviality freely. It was as if the majority of the children had known the staff most of their lives and the effect of that was displayed in their behaviour, which helped to put me at ease. I will always remember my first lesson; I panicked and was reduced to tears at the thought of not being able to write like the other children. I watched nervously as Mr Parker scripted beautifully written sentences on the blackboard, enabling every child in the room to copy each word perfectly into their notepads, but I had spent so much time away from school that I couldn't even read what had been written, let alone write it down. So I cried like a baby wondering what I was going to do next. I didn't worry only for that day but for the days that followed, as I knew I had to learn everything my classmates had already learnt, but I wasn't sure I was capable of doing that. Having been left to cry for some time Mr Parker removed me from his classroom and introduced me to Mrs Hurst, who taught the younger children of the school. She was made aware that I couldn't read and write and explained in simple terms that all she wanted me to do was to try and print

3

some simple words. She was kind and somehow able to put my fears at rest; for that day at least. Each day I struggled to do the work but nothing looked like it should have, especially for someone of my age. Every day my confidence took a battering as I slipped deeper and deeper into my shell. I spoke to and played with no-one, eventually appreciating the little time Tyrone spent tormenting me in the playground. At other schools I had been ridiculed for many things, including my inability to read and write, but never had I been playfully tormented for my good qualities. This was how I knew that the children from Ashford were somewhat different. It seemed they had seen so many Outrake children come and go that they had a greater understanding of the problems we carried upon our shoulders, which enabled us to fit in more easily.

Looking back at that first day I remember seeing a lot of good qualities among the children of Ashford, but up until now I had never given much thought to them or their lives. Now I sit and wonder if I could have accepted so many dispirited children coming and going in and out of my life the way they accepted us coming in and out of theirs. I built up quite a friendship with Tyrone, although I got angry with him on most days. This was usually more to do with my own irritability towards the opposite sex than anything else. I had an unusual amount of respect for him for he was the only male I had ever met that didn't frighten or abuse me in some way. Tyrone never did what was expected of him but he seemed to be the most light-hearted character of Ashford community, so I knew I would never forget him. Then there was his younger brother, Carl. He didn't begin to attend Ashford Juniors until I was due to leave, but for the short time I remained I tried to treat him as well as his brother had treated me. Carl wasn't as robust as Tyrone and yet he had the same excitable giddiness that made me feel a little high-spirited when he was around. His appearance was much the same as Tyrone's except that his hair was a lighter brown and a little shorter. However, it seemed that both boys were a little rough around the edges yet rather handsome; an attribute that was seldom discussed among children of the yesteryear.

When I left Ashford Junior School, I must admit I shed a few tears as I had become quite accustomed to being part of a community that was so relaxed and calm; far better than anything I had ever known before. It was a small part of my life that I didn't want to forget and felt a little cheated when I realised that my move was inevitable. I found it difficult to understand why each time I began to settle down I was uprooted and moved on. Everything I enjoyed and the people I liked were all cast aside to make room for my progress. Being a child in care I thought very little about moving from one place to another but it was abandoning my friends that I didn't like. It was only a few years later when I had left the Outrake children's home that I truly understood the changes that occurred in me each time I was moved. My life changed so often that I became more aware of the people I left behind and so began to guard against getting too close to anyone. My exterior was pretty tough by the time I had left school, although occasionally I made the mistake of allowing certain individuals to slip through the cracks; I only experienced heartache and suffering. Despite the continuous moves and changes in my life, I vowed I would never forget anyone who had been good to me. So when I remember all the people I left behind, I find it difficult to estimate the total value of such good friends. I had not considered myself very lucky as a child. Having been abused, I suppose I even felt a little sorry for myself, but when I put faces to all the names I recall, I realise I wasn't as badly done to as some of the children I was in care with. When I think about my sister, Lorraine, who displayed so much sadness in her face, continually suffered the pain of nervous eczema and walked with a permanent stoop because of the frequent bullying she suffered, I could cry for her. Knowing how badly even I treated her at times when the going got tough and it was a fight of the fittest - I fought and won - I should beg for her forgiveness!

—⚶—

CHAPTER 2

Devastation

Many things have happened during my life which I know I should think about more often, but sometimes I find it easier just to try and forget them. I have some memories that are permanently fixed in my mind and no matter how much I try to shake them off they stay with me, reminding me that during parts of my childhood I was the lucky one!

I was aged fourteen when I first met my friend, Denise Stafford. She was absolutely beautiful, confident and full of the joys of spring and at first I admired her for both her looks and her qualities. We attended Ravensdale School in Mansfield where we became bosom pals, seldom going anywhere without each other until she became pregnant and was forced to leave school. Then our lives became so different that we had nothing to talk about and I had to face the fact that we were more like chalk and cheese than anything else. We still saw each other but drifted apart when she began to go out with the boy who fathered her child. I recall visiting her at her bedsit just after she gave birth to her little girl, but as the years drifted by I went my own way and Denise settled down like she had always wanted. At school she never spoke about anything else and I remember getting a little bored with her continuous chattering about the men in her life and what she did with them. I put up with the things that she did and the stuff that she spoke about simply because I was a new pupil at her school and had difficulty making friends. I suppose, looking back, her personality was somewhat different to mine and although our appearances were similar, we had very little in common. But like all teenagers we dressed in identical clothing and the topic of our conversations were boys, music and fashion. Then I remember we parted company and I didn't see her for a good few years.

I was in my late twenties when I saw her again. Our meeting was extraordinary. I had two beautiful children of my own and was expecting twins, but as we spoke she seemed a little agitated to be travelling on the same bus as me. I felt disappointed when she got off at the earliest convenience as I had missed her and hoped that we could rekindle our friendship, but she was in so much of a hurry she got off the bus without saying goodbye or even exchanging telephone numbers. When I arrived home I mentioned it to my husband, Paul, and asked him if he knew her, but when he said he didn't I ceased talking about her and, with each day that passed, any hope of seeing her again gradually faded from my mind. When I gave birth to the twins, all the excitement of two new babies replaced any dwindling thoughts I had of her and I moved on with my life. Time seemed to pass quickly and within no time at all the twins had reached their first birthday and I hadn't seen her in all that time. Then one day I heard people talking in the street about an incident that had occurred within our local area. The name Denise Chilternam hadn't registered at first, but when I visited my mother I was devastated when she explained to me that Denise

Chilternam was my friend from school. She showed me an article from the local newspaper that featured Denise and I almost passed out. Her face was so disfigured I didn't recognise her, but the article spoke of the most horrendous attack that she and her children had suffered. It was apparent that she had married and was known as Denise Chilternam. Unfortunately she was in the wrong place at the wrong time and had faced an appalling attack that had devastating results. From that moment on I regretted not having seen her after that initial meeting on the bus and have wondered many times if I had, would it have changed the course of her life? I cannot think that anything she may have done would have warranted such an attack and have shed many tears while thinking about her lying in a pool of blood in what was supposed to be the safety of her own home. I have wondered to this very day how anyone could have done that; knowing that the severity of their attack could have killed her. I cannot think of anything positive to say about a person who is capable of causing such devastation and can only think that it was by the grace of God that she survived. I guess she will always carry the scars of that attack and I take my hat off to her, for she is the bravest person I have ever met. Sometimes I find it very difficult to understand why some people live in such comfortable carefree worlds while others, through no fault of their own, suffer at the hands of others and then spend the rest of their lives picking up the pieces that they are left with. I suppose it's easy for some people to turn a blind eye to the things that don't affect them and say, 'life is what we make it', but I wonder how many of us are really convinced of that.

Until four years ago I had never met a single soul who really understood what devastation and trauma like that could cause, then I met my counsellor, Clive Powell, a man with so much understanding he made a huge impact on my life almost immediately. After a long period of anxiety depression, I suffered a breakdown which affected every aspect of my life and I found it virtually impossible to live with the constant torment of my past. When I first met Clive, I had no way of knowing how things would turn out. For years I had struggled daily from the effect of phobias and self-doubt which isolated me from the outside world. It was a case of having suffered so long that I accepted my situation as the norm and was convinced that my life was almost at an end. After previously seeing other counsellors, I had convinced myself that rehabilitation was beyond my reach and I began to lose any hope of recovery, but at the outset of my treatment with Clive he prepared me for the long extensive sessions he was convinced I needed. However I was no ordinary client and I knew at the same time that I must test his ability to cope with the traumatized sessions that we were both about to experience. I didn't find it easy to unload fitting descriptions of myself being sexually abused by my oldest brother, John, when I was only a small child, and I found no pleasure in informing Clive of my extraordinary upbringing, but he was my one final hope. So, in desperation I gave it my all, hoping that he could give me back my life.

During my first session I watched him like a hawk, looking for any signs of weakness and re-evaluating everything he said. I was terribly nervous but his reassurance seemed to calm me and it was my intuition that told me that he was the right person to confide in. But first of all I had to find out how he felt about child abuse, rape, attempted murder and even death. These were just some of the memories that had haunted me

all of my life. I needed to be sure that he was capable
of listening to my whole life story without making
me feel embarrassed or uncomfortable, without passing
judgment or showing repulsion, but most of all I had to
know that he believed me. As his client I felt it was as
much my right to analyse him as it was his to analyse me.
Fortunately he had no scruples about it, so it was at that
point he earned a little of my respect. After countless
questions and unequivocal remarks, I saw a man who
wasn't easily put off by my probing and sarcasm.
Someone who seemed qualified enough to answer any of
my dubious questions without showing any signs of
disapproval. Eventually I began to trust him and spoke
openly about my abusive childhood and, like so many
times before, I unloaded one hell of a story! It was
difficult to repeat all the repulsive memories I had of the
violation of my bare flesh and it got much worse before
it got better. The difficulty was that I couldn't accept that
I was the little girl 'Molly', who had suffered so much
abuse, but somehow he got me to drift through my life
right up to my teenage years, giving a full account of all
the abuse that I had suffered. Although I began to trust
him a little, I found it difficult to keep eye contact with
him and found myself regularly checking that he wasn't
showing signs of disbelief or embarrassment like so
many others had in the past. He remained calm and
relaxed throughout each session. Although I felt terribly
nervous, I had to admit I had never met anyone like him.
Occasionally I wondered if he was really listening to me
and I would fire an unexpected question at him hoping
to catch him unprepared, but I was surprised he
remained focussed for so long. I remember there were
times when I felt sorry for him too and asked if he had

anyone to unload to. I don't know why I felt he had problems of his own, just occasionally I sensed a kind of sadness within him. Sometimes I was taken aback a little with his replies. For some reason I hadn't expected him to admit needing anyone, but it was those little things that made me realise that he was human too. By the time I had got around to talking about my adult years, I felt lucky to have met him and had built up so much trust in him that I could tell him anything. Our sessions were not always filled with doom and gloom. At times he laughed so heartily when I made fun and often made jokes of his own. Then I realised how lucky I was and noticed that the only time that I smiled was once a fortnight during our hourly sessions, which by that time he had become a very important part of my life. At that stage I couldn't see myself coping without counselling and the worry of some day having to caused me even more anxiety, but he put my mind at ease regarding that too. I had never spoken to anyone else about my horrendous childhood in such great detail. Yet there stood a man who knew every ghastly detail there was to know. It seemed the more progress I made, the easier my life became.

When I felt down and out of my mind, I managed to cut myself off from every individual I cared about, not realising how much they were hurting. For almost ten years I allowed them to suffer while I wallowed in silence. No-one could reach me. Then I met Clive, who cared enough to bring me back from the anomalous world I had entered into. I found myself sharing memories with him that had not left my mind in forty years; memories that had haunted my childhood and plagued my future, even problems that arose within my own family. I found myself going down pathways

I hadn't dared to tread and cried both tears of sadness and of joy, and within time I sighed deeply with relief. It took me two whole years to open up and tell him my story but never once did he show any signs of repugnance. Today I still suffer from the effects of anxiety and occasionally I make a journey to Lincoln to visit him. Only now he has become my mentor and my friend, as I have gained enough confidence to move on to far more challenging things. I still struggle from day to day with life as we know it but I plough through, hoping the decisions I make are the right ones.

Since my breakdown I have spoken to many people about the effects of counselling and oddly enough there are still those who consider it pointless, and I suppose up to me meeting Clive I was very much of the same opinion but when I walked into his room for the very first time I realised the quotation, 'A problem shared is a problem halved' was definitely correct.

—◌—

CHAPTER 3

A Cry for Help

I recall when I was a young girl, I feared everyone who suffered from mental or nervous disorders. Then when I finally reached my teenage years, I became inquisitive and watched films on television that terrified me, solely because they contained sketches of insanity or psychosis. I couldn't understand why some doctors went onto become psychologists and psychiatrists. But when I fell ill myself, I looked at things differently. Although I wasn't without fear, I had a greater understanding of the disorders that once terrified me and pitied the people who suffered from them. Instead of walking around with my eyes shut and my mind closed, I began to concentrate on everything that was taboo. Human lack of understanding and thoughtless actions made me realise how great our ignorance was of illnesses that affected the mind. I began to wonder what it was about these illnesses that terrified us so, but I had no answers. All I knew was that my own embarrassment caused me to suffer in silence, hoping that my grip on reality would return by itself without the aid of medical staff or advice from a doctor. I suffered unnecessarily. Then I realised my sickness was niggling its way around my mind, lessening my chances of recovery. I first sought professional advice when I was aged twenty-nine. I wasn't sure what was wrong, only that it affected everything that I did. I hadn't been well since the birth of the twins in 1987, but for five long years every doctor I had approached seemed baffled by my symptoms. I suffered drastically from something that had been labelled, 'an imaginary illness', and failed to cope with everyday tasks. Although I fought long and hard, I lost the battle to care for my youngest children appropriately. Although I managed to care for my nine-year-old son, Ian, the Social Services found thirteen-month-old twins, Kyle and Allishia, a placement with foster parents. Having my eldest daughter, Cheniels' best interests at heart, I approached my ex-partner Nigel and asked him if he would mind caring for her until I recovered from whatever it was I was suffering. Having lived within the care system for a large part of my life, I knew enough about the Social Services to know that I was going to have a battle on my hands when I was well enough to bring my children home. So it seemed logical at the time only to allow them to care for my youngest children; the ones least likely to remember being separated from me when they got older. The courts had already granted Nigel access to Cheniel following our break-up, so I saw no reason why he shouldn't care for her while I was ill. I approached him hoping I could rely on him and thought he would understand, but I later found that every person I trusted turned against me, which made my and the children's lives even more difficult. I had never imagined life without my children and wasn't sure I could live without them. Many times I felt like giving up and often contemplated taking my own life, but the very thought of leaving them without a mother gave me the strength to keep on fighting. I cried continually at the thought of leaving them somewhere they didn't want to be, but I was powerless and, according to the Social Services, didn't have the right to move them. It broke my heart to hear four-year-old Cheniel cry out for me in the street each time she saw me. Until then it hadn't fully registered how much she was hurting. Despite my ill health, I knew I owed it to her to remain strong. It was from that moment I battled with my inner self, knowing that if I didn't have the strength to fight and get well, I would never bring her home. Nigel had already accused me of abandonment and did his utmost to prove to the authorities that I wasn't interested in her or her wellbeing, and I was so ill I had lost all my communication skills and failed drastically in any attempts that I made to prove otherwise. I just couldn't make them understand I was incapable of abandoning her. I repeatedly told them how much I loved her, but no matter how hard I tried, they only believed what they wanted to believe. Had they looked deeper than my tired skin, they would have seen a caring mother who loves her children with all her heart; a mother who was capable of giving so much more than just materialistic things but all the love and affection a child needed.

For five long years I battled with the Social Services, barristers and judges, but it was difficult trying to explain a disabling illness that even doctors couldn't diagnose. I suffered memory lapses, panic attacks and lacked concentration. Sometimes I was unable to function at all. I trembled from head to foot and the pounding of my heart felt so loud that I was certain it could be heard for miles. I was often told that my appearance resembled a ninety-year-old woman, but I fought hard to keep on top of things for the sake of my children. At times my life became so difficult it seemed the easiest option would be to give in to the demons that taunted me, only to find in my moment of weakness I suffered even more terrifying bouts of panic.

While I suffered a long hard journey of guilt, I went from doctor to doctor, hospital to hospital, searching for a diagnosis of underlying symptoms. The sight of a hysterical mother quaking in her boots, running around like a headless chicken, was treated with the contempt it deserved and I suffered miserably for a few more years until a diagnosis was found. I was told so often that I was suffering from stress and the chances were it was the twins that caused it… something I never expected to hear. But upon visiting Dr Morgan at Spilsby surgery in Lincolnshire, after countless appointments he gave me back my optimism and offered me every chance to pull through. He was the one doctor who eventually listened to me without passing judgment or doubting my word. I had never been for a brain scan before, so was terrified of visiting the hospital. Certain there was something more wrong, I feared the results and prayed to God every night to spare me. Time seemed to stand still for a while as I desperately struggled with the thought of having a disease from which I might die. But when the date for my scan arrived, I struggled to make the eighty mile journey to The Queens Medical at Nottingham, where I was seen by Dr Godwin Austin, the chief neurologist. He was kind and considerate and gave me a complete examination of the nervous system, then sent me for an EEG. I was devastated when he prescribed me anticonvulsant drugs for epilepsy, but at the same time I assumed my worries were all over and for a second or two I began to think positively - until he suggested an MRI scan. He was unsure whether or not my symptoms indicated Parkinson's disease or Multiple Sclerosis. I didn't know whether to laugh or cry; lots of things had crossed my mind but I must admit neither of these had. I held very little knowledge of these diseases and didn't understand what any of them involved. But I suppose the impact of such information was lessened by the thought of being able to fight for the custody of my children, knowing that I could actually confirm the name of at least one of my disabling diseases. I hadn't a clue how I was going to prove to the authorities that I was fit to take care of them and I wasn't really sure that I could, but one thing I did know, they were desperate to come home and I was going to do all that I could to bring them home. I was their mother and it was their right to live with me. As my medication began to take effect, I became far more controlled than I had been for years. Although some of my symptoms remained, I thanked God for the peace that those pills gave to me.

Finally I regained my rational mind and I began the fight of a lifetime. I remember the months that followed were really difficult. Despite all the ups and downs trying to regulate my medication, I registered my application with the courts and began the fight to bring my children home. It was a long drawn out battle and, although I had always tried to be a good mother, I was the first to admit that there had been times when I could have done better, but in a desperate attempt to save my children I applied to the Nottingham High Court begging for their return. When I was invited to explain where things had gone wrong, I was chauffeured to the courthouse by the children's social worker, Rachel Carter, who literally begged me to sign them over before we had even reached the courthouse. But I had come too far for that. I didn't consider it to be in their best interests, but she failed to understand that. It was at that moment that I realised why I had lost every ounce of respect for her. Suddenly I remembered it was her who had refused me help when I needed it most, who treated me with so much contempt when I had begged her to give me respite. Now she had no qualms about pressing me to sign forms before we reached the courthouse, forms which allowed her to take my children without as much as a fight. Luckily I wasn't as naive as she thought and I refused point blank. On that day I sat before a very sympathetic judge, who understood that sometimes parents do become ill and occasionally do have the need for respite. It was just unfortunate for me and my children that members of the Mansfield Social Services department persecuted me for it. Although it seemed at times that all the odds were against me I fought long and hard for what I thought was right and regained custody of my babies, Kyle and Allishia.

When I walked away from the courthouse holding just three of my children's futures in my hands, I realised what a stupid mistake I had made by trusting Nigel. The one person I had hoped that I could trust had deceived me. Although we had an understanding that he would allow Cheniel to come home when I was well enough to take care of her, he had lied. Honesty was never one of his better qualities and he never really thought of anyone but himself. But I gave him the benefit of the doubt, not realising that he wouldn't place her welfare and happiness before his own. I sought legal advice from a solicitor, who in turn engaged a barrister on my behalf, but two years passed before I was allowed a hearing in the high court and already time was against me, but I persevered and remained optimistic at all times. At that time I had every faith in our legal system and believed that they would do Cheniel justice, but I found that there was more to it than just telling the truth. First of all I had to prove how much I loved her, how much she wanted to come home, and if it was for all the right reasons. Would it be in her best interests? Or was I really an unfit mother? Should it be my legal right to be considered more appropriate to take care of her, just because I'm her mother? Nothing was made simple. The hearing was made so difficult I barely got through it. I had never been made to feel so humiliated in all my life. Suddenly it had become against the law to be ill and I was almost held in 'contempt of court' for trying to defend myself against the lies that Nigel told on oath. The whole procedure was like a game of charades. It had nothing much to do with Cheniel's welfare or happiness. The authorities seemed to amalgamate and the history of my abusive childhood was held against me, like it had been all my life, and my poor innocent daughter paid a very heavy price for it. So I asked myself, where was the justice in that?

After numerous appearances before our judges, I made yet another application to the courts but, despite all my efforts, I could not beat the system. Nigel ruined every chance I had of bringing her home and, despite her continued pleas, he insisted on keeping her with him. She cried a mountain of tears each time I left her and never abstained from urging me to fight for her again. But I was literally exhausted and the stress of it all was beginning to show. Yet she was my little girl and I loved her with all my heart, and for that reason alone

I carried on. It was inevitable that I would eventually suffer for it.

I'd had a lot to contend with over the years and my health had gone up and down like a yo-yo. I tried to keep on top of things but I continued to suffer terribly with my nerves, the result of permanently trying to maintain dignity and self-respect for the sake of my children. I knew once the high court had made a decision, it was virtually impossible to get them to change it back. Cheniel was almost twelve years old when I made my final application to the courts, and then the judge told me, 'If Cheniel is unhappy, she will grow her own boots and start walking.' He was right, at the age of fourteen, Cheniel left Nigel's house just weeks after he had abandoned her to live with another woman and her children. Luckily Cheniel still had me. Eventually she made her way back to me and, like so many other children who bear the injustices of our courts; she spent years picking up the pieces that she was left with. Now she has grown and in her twenties she still suffers from the trauma of a broken home and spends a lot of her time wishing things had been different. The bond between Cheniel and her siblings has never returned to its best. The separation caused so much doubt and uncertainty that on occasions they find it extremely difficult to tolerate each other. Kyle and Allishia have now flown the nest and have made their lives their own. Although at times they each face difficulties, they remain strong and climb every hurdle they come across. Ian has been a treasure to us all, picking up pieces that I have dropped, holding the family together until once again I was well enough to do it myself. Many times I have wondered what

I would have done during the times I couldn't have managed without him. Now as a man with children, I look on him with so much pride, as I do all my children. And I thank God for each and every one of them.

At times I have found it difficult to look back and accept the mistakes I have made, but now I do it with ease, knowing that I did my best and from my best came four of God's beautiful children.

—⚬—

CHAPTER 4

Against All Odds

I remember there were many times during my life when I couldn't bear to think about getting married or having children, but my life changed once I had given birth to Ian. I was aged twenty, a single mother - and overjoyed. The very thought of having someone to care for seemed to be all I that I wanted. I didn't find motherhood easy but then I didn't expect I would. I was so proud to be his mother and put every ounce of love that I felt for him into taking care of him. I protected him and, no matter what, I always put him first. Five years on I gave birth to my daughter Cheniel. It was amazing, although there was a part of me that still feared the responsibility that came with little girls, I was as much in love with her as I was with Ian and instantly knew even against all odds I would try to be a good mother. I had never experienced having parents in the correct sense so I didn't feel it was important for Ian and Cheniel to have both a mother and father. I knew I was more than capable of taking care of them and felt extremely protective towards them, so I found it almost impossible to share the joy I felt for them with anyone else. But when they began to feature their fathers, I gave a considerable amount of thought to them and wondered how it must feel for a man to father a child they couldn't help to raise. Having been raised in a care home for the largest part of my life, I found parenting and relationships immensely difficult. My life had not been as straightforward as most people's so I lacked understanding and found men to be the most complex creatures I had ever come across. I didn't expect any of them to understand me, but at the same time I didn't expect to develop feelings for any of them either. When I first met Ian's father, Paul Frith, he treated me with so much respect that I couldn't help but like him. I hadn't known him long before he introduced me to his parents and, although I should have felt out of my depth, I didn't. So when they invited me to their home for tea I accepted without hesitation. Although they lived in the more refined area of Mansfield I couldn't wait to visit them, but when I did I was so shy I could barely hold my head up let alone hold a conversation. But Paul was so thoughtful he often interrupted their conversations and spoke for me; even so, I still found it difficult to communicate with them. I wasn't used to people being considerate towards me so when his feelings began to show I panicked at the thought of being trapped in a suffocating relationship. Nothing seemed to go right at that time. I wasn't sure what Paul or his family thought of me or whether I was capable of fulfilling any of their expectations so I walked away from him, freeing myself of any unnecessary ties. A few months later my doctor confirmed that I was pregnant. I wasn't surprised as I knew on the night that I slept with him that there was a slight possibility and yet I still walked out, knowing that there was no turning back. Ian was almost two years old before Paul found out about him. Although he occasionally visited my home, he never questioned me about Ian and never made me feel uncomfortable while he was around. I lived in a very small council house at Ravensdale in Mansfield for a while, struggling to feed and clothe Ian but never once made any demands on Paul or his family. I cared for Ian to the best of my ability and never ever regretted his existence. I tried to come to terms with what had happened between me and my family and tried my best to get on with Mother. She gave me the impression that she loved Ian as much as I did, although she regularly reminded me that he was her thirteenth grandchild and that she believed that that was unlucky for some. It was only when Ian was born so close to her birthday that I felt that she was genuinely proud of him. I saw things in her that I had never seen before and hardly recognized her as being the same mother I had as a child. As Ian grew, so did the relationship between Mother and me. I found it difficult to remember everything that had happened in the past and sometimes I wondered if I had been dreaming the horrid scenes that regularly taunted my brain. But then I received visits from the Social Services team, investigating complaints about me – lodged by my own mother. Fortunately her reports were always unfounded, but the hurt she caused was as painful as the terrible memories I had of her. I never got to the bottom of the accusations she made against me but as the years passed I learned that they were strongly connected to the arrest of my brother, John, when he sexually abused me as a child. She had always found it impossible to accept that he was a paedophile and never forgave me for being one of his victims. I was still very young and forgave her for everything she had said, only to be accused of something different soon after. At times I felt sorry for her. I knew she always believed that John was innocent and this was her way of repaying me for proving otherwise. It was only when I met my new boyfriend, Keith Fraser, that she stopped accusing me of neglecting Ian.

Keith was twenty years my senior and seemed a very fair and honest man. Although he showed a lot of respect towards Mother, he never allowed her to call or belittle me. He made it clear to my family that the only thing that he ever expected from them was respect and he expected the same for me. Because of his forthright manner, Mother seemed to get on with him pretty well and respected everything he did. I first met Keith in the Red Lion public house at Mansfield. Although it was reputed to be a gay pub, it seemed to be the place where everyone wanted to be. I first started going in there because the only gay woman I knew seemed to be far friendlier than any other person I had ever met and certainly knew how to enjoy herself. It was the first public place where I felt safe, and after three months it felt like home from home. I recall when Paul Frith and I broke up, I began to question my sexuality and realised that I felt much more comfortable in the presence of gays of either sex. When I was a young girl I had often wondered about my sexuality as I had been attracted to females ever since the age of fourteen, but I suppose like many of us I kept it to myself wondering if there was something radically wrong with me. I never spoke about my feelings to anyone, simply because I didn't trust anyone enough to voice them. I was aged twenty-one before I experienced my first encounter with a woman and found it to be far more intense than anything I had ever known. When I first met Jo, she typically resembled a handsome young man dressed in a white shirt and black leather trousers.

She featured one of the better looking boys I knew at school; although she appeared to be very butch, there was still a strong femininity about her. I was positively sure she was male but couldn't help being attracted to the feminine side of her. It was only when I questioned my best friend about her brother that I realised I had been deluded. I felt very embarrassed at the thought of being attracted to a homosexual but, despite that, I couldn't drag myself away from her. After many weeks I finally plucked up the courage to accept her invitation to a night out in the town. I was utterly surprised when she admitted that she had been attracted to me for weeks but as I was considered to be heterosexual, she feared rejection and put it off. Although she had previously slept with women, she was my first and despite the mixed feelings I had about my own sexuality, my affair with her felt so right. It was at that point of my life that I began to pay attention to my own inner feelings and, strange as it seemed, it felt like the most natural thing in the world to be loved by her.

Ever since I was a teenager I had been wrestling with the thought of being gay and yet I knew I was also attracted to boys. I remember as far back as the Outrake, I regularly masturbated fantasizing about making love to a woman and later, when I slept with a man, I found it impossible to orgasm unless I fantasized about making love to that same woman. All those strange thoughts and uncertainties created so much confusion in me; I wasn't sure what I was. But when I met Jo, I thought I had finally come to terms with who I was and accepted what I thought was the most natural feeling in the world. But when I met Keith he helped me to understand the reason why I was like I was and then I realised, the abuse that

I had suffered as a child had caused me so much doubt and uncertainty that I was left questioning my sexuality. I recall Keith was so much like Jo that I was instantly attracted to him. Although he was strong and attractive, he too had a feminine quality about him which I liked. Having Italian blood he was the most attractive man I had ever seen so I fell for him hook, line and sinker. I allowed him to get underneath my skin almost immediately but despite our lengthy relationship I found that my feelings for Jo soon got in the way and I yo-yoed from one to another, causing embarrassing situations between the three of us. Although Keith was a self-confessed bi-sexual, he couldn't accept the fact that I was attracted to Jo and became outrageously jealous of her. Within no time at all they became rivals and fought over what they considered to be theirs. I found myself in the position of choosing between the two of them but, because I had feelings for both, it was far more difficult than I expected. Eventually I chose what I perceived to be 'normal' but, even after trying to re-establish our relationship, Keith and I ran into so many other troubles that I found living with him almost impossible. I had never figured him as being the vengeful type but in time I discovered that he was sleeping around, keeping me in abeyance until he felt it was time to forgive me. I was never able to understand his logic. He slept around with both men and women and yet still couldn't accept me being attracted to Jo, so I knew at that point that I would never stay with him. Our relationship was so confusing and, although I thought I loved him, I found myself constantly battling with him, trying to justify everything that I did. Although Keith thought I would never leave him, after telling him I had met someone else I packed my belongings for the very last time and said goodbye. I was almost twenty-three years old.

Although it wasn't the most considerate thing to do, I arranged for a man I had previously met at a nightclub to pick me up from Keith's door. I was glad when he did as I couldn't wait to leave. I had arranged for Arch Simpson to pick me up on a Sunday afternoon after I had confessed and explained my intentions to Keith. It wasn't a confrontational break-up but I left just as I always thought I would, in good spirits and still friends. He kissed me at the door before I left but I held myself rigid and tried to switch off so that I didn't crumble in his arms. I was so sure that I loved him and knew that he loved me, but the time had come for me to move on. I couldn't stay. I had to move on and put all of that behind me; he knew that.

My life with Arch began the moment I walked out of the door. I had been totally honest with the pair of them and couldn't see any harm in leaving one to move in with the other. Keith seemed rather upset that I had allowed Arch to pick me up from outside his front door and couldn't understand why Arch, the perpetrator, had insisted on it. It seemed that Arch wanted me to prove that my relationship with Keith was over before he was willing to commit himself. I felt awful walking away from Keith like that. We had been such good friends in the past and, although we had been through hell and back trying to get our relationship off the ground, after almost two years just when we thought we had everything going for us my past came back to haunt me and I felt trapped. It became a regular pattern, moving in with someone new and moving on within two years. I had always hated the thought of being known inside out and the longer I was with someone; the more they probed into a part of my life I was trying to hide. So much had happened in the past, I felt sure that if any of them had found out about Little Molly they would have hated me anyway. So I left before they got to know me. I had feelings but kept them to myself – I thought it was best that way.

—⁓—

CHAPTER 5

Betrayed

I picked Ian up from my mother's and stopped off at my house to collect a few toys and clothes, then set off with Arch on a journey to Chesterfield where he lived with his two small children, Adam and Nicola. I was a little apprehensive about going to live with him as most of my family, including my brother, John, still lived in Chesterfield. However, when we arrived there I realised that Arch lived way out of town in one of the most beautiful rural parts of Chesterfield. Nevertheless I was still uncertain about going back to live there. It took a little over an hour to reach Chesterfield and a further ten minutes to arrive at Arch's four-bedroomed semi in the village of Wingerworth. It was referred to as one of the most sought-after areas and I could certainly see why. Some of the houses were exquisite and the surrounding countryside was breathtaking. I was pleased to see that some of the areas of Chesterfield were left unspoiled, which made re-settling there a little easier. Having lived in Mansfield for some time, I had simply forgotten how beautiful my home town really was.

I felt really uneasy when I first walked into the house and it took me quite some time to get used to his children but I found that once Carol, their nanny, had returned from her weekend away things began to fall into place and she made me feel more at ease. Carol was eighteen and more my age so I felt quite relaxed when she was around. Although she did most of the housework, I immediately volunteered to do the cooking and we seemed to work in harmony taking care of the children, Ian, Adam and Nicola. Ian seemed very happy and I was quite surprised how well he adjusted. He was a year younger than Adam, Arch's youngest, so got on quite well with him. Adam was almost four when we met and had been attending nursery school for some time. His seven-year-old sister, Nicola, was attending Wingerworth Primary School which was situated next to the nursery but, despite them being extremely well nurtured, I could see that they desperately lacked the care of a mother. Arch was quite open about the break-up of his marriage and his relationship with their mother. He spent hours talking to me about her. It was apparent that she had become reliant on morphine following a major operation. Being a nurse she had every opportunity to feed the habit she desperately tried to control, but eventually it destroyed all of their lives, leaving the children traumatised and Arch heartbroken. It took him years to pick up the pieces and even then it was obvious to me that there was a huge empty space in their lives which needed to be filled and, although I was so young, I fitted into that space quite naturally.

Nicola was beautiful. She had the most amazing blue eyes and long blonde hair; every inch a princess. Adam, on the other hand, had big brown eyes and a mass of blond curls that swept loosely over his brow. He spoke extremely well for his age and was already showing signs of intellect; a chip off the old block, I always used to say.

It felt like the most natural thing in the world to love them. I loved Arch and I loved our children dearly and the most amazing thing was that I loved them all equally.

Arch was twelve years my senior and had previously spent a considerable amount of time with the Royal Air Force, but since he had married and had children his life had changed dramatically. Although he still worked, he told me that it wasn't a job that he enjoyed and that he found it difficult to maintain the standards that he had been used to. I always remember him worrying about the children and their needs and occasionally he would burst into tears when he thought there was no-one there for him. I knew if it hadn't been for the fact that he played rugby, he wouldn't have had anything to look forward to. He treated our children well. Being a man of exceptional intelligence, his ability to think and understand them seemed far better than my instinct but together we worked hard at being a family and for a while it worked exceptionally well. I was happier than I had ever been in my life and really thought that I had met the man I would eventually marry. But then the company whom Arch worked for went out of business and he found himself unemployed - a situation that he had never encountered before. He hated the thought of registering unemployed but, determined to pay the mortgage and see that our children didn't go without; he accepted all kinds of cheap labour. Unable to find suitable employment to meet his level of education, he drove long haul for a friend just so he didn't have to sign on the dole. It wasn't a well paid job but Chesterfield wasn't the best area in which to find suitable employment either. It was full of factories and mining villages and eventually he gave up hope of ever finding work. Being the intellectual type I doubt he would have survived shift work beneath the ground. Arch had this growing fear of being forced into the situation of having to sell his house and move away, so he gave Carol the opportunity to leave and paid her up to date. I took over the housework and all the chores, but Arch became so disheartened when he realised he could no longer achieve the standards that he was used to and eventually lost all hope and suffered a terrible bout of depression. I didn't understand what was going on in his mind or why it seemed so important to him to keep the status that he had acquired over the years. Apart from keeping house and taking care of the children, I couldn't help him. His expectations were far too high, so when the going got tough I got scared and found it too difficult to cope with a man who had previously shown such strength and determination but had now weakened and solely relied on me to take care of him, his home and his family.

I was a young girl in my early twenties and knew so little about depression or mortgages, and failed to understand what it took to put things right. I knew I was failing him and, on top of everything else, I found out that I was expecting his baby. I was so scared to tell him as I knew the timing was completely wrong and would only add to his troubles. So I began to go downhill myself, frequently losing my temper and crying at the drop of a hat. I considered another abortion, but I had already terminated one pregnancy when I left Keith so certainly didn't want another. When I made love to Arch, there wasn't a single moment that I didn't feel special and I loved him so much I would have died for him - but I wasn't prepared to take the life of another baby. When Arch began to recover, I showed signs of early pregnancy, vomiting every morning, looking pale and wan with worry. For reasons I will never understand, I planned to end our relationship. Arch was devastated and took an overdose. It was the first time that he had done anything like that and it made me realise that I had destroyed yet another life. It seemed that everyone I came into contact with was ruined by my unpredictable ways. I couldn't understand why I was leaving him; I hadn't worked out any particular reason for doing so. All I knew was that the baby I was carrying was part of him and I wanted it more than anything. It felt so right, I was willing to forfeit my life with him to keep it. At that time there seemed to be no other way, so I moved out of his house to pursue a life with Ian and the baby.

I moved into a council property close to his home and, because he didn't want me to move too far away, he decorated and furnished it for me. We parted as friends but when he started going out with Janice, he changed dramatically. He had known her for some time and, although I had only seen her twice while I was still with him, I believed that she lured him away from me. What I didn't envisage was the two of them staying together. I was almost four months pregnant when I saw him again and, although I still hadn't told him about the baby, he became very angry when he saw me with my new boyfriend, Nigel. I had never seen him look so angry and was shocked to see him that way. He told me that he knew I was pregnant and tore open my jacket which was so carefully disguising my bump. Then he knocked me to the ground. I cried because I still loved him, but there was something inside my head that wouldn't allow me to tell him so. I wanted to be with him but the guiding force that I had always been ruled by wouldn't allow it.

It seemed that I avoided happiness at all costs. I left him at the side of the road, heartbroken and full of tears. I called at my home to collect a few clothes for Ian and myself; once again I felt that I needed to get away. I couldn't bear to think about Arch with Janice so I went to stay with my sister, Carol, for a while. She was pretty good at getting me drunk to take my mind off things and, because she never liked Arch, she did all that she could to stop me from going back to him. I spent the next five months building a relationship with Nigel, who wasn't half the man Arch was. He was someone who fitted the description of a male chauvinist and proved to be the biggest mistake of my life.

I heard nothing more from Arch until I gave birth to our beautiful daughter, Cheniel, when to my surprise he appeared at the hospital with a huge bouquet of flowers. A small card was attached with the inscription: 'To Marie and baby with love from the father.' I was instantly taken aback and instead of showing my appreciation, I became angry and cried. I was terrified of Nigel seeing Arch or the flowers, just the very thought of Arch being around would have angered him terribly. Nigel wasn't the most understanding person and I feared him more than anything. I immediately had the flowers removed and told the nurse on duty that under no circumstances was she to allow Arch in to see me. Even at that point I knew how much I loved him, but couldn't bring myself to accept it. I had done wrong but wouldn't say so. It seemed that I was fighting against something which felt so natural yet I still couldn't understand why.

I didn't stay with Nigel. I found out that he had been seeing several women behind my back and his violence became so unbearable that I had to consider what was best for my children. After suffering numerous beatings and regular abuse, our relationship ended in the magistrates' courts with an order to remove him from my home. I applied for custody of my children and fortunately his violence was taken into account and an order was made in my favour. We separated only to see each other again when he applied for access to the children. I tried to look at our situation sensitively and consider Nigel's and my children's feelings. He had allowed Cheniel to take his name, so I supposed he had every right to see her and he made sure that those rights were put into place. Despite having knowledge of his previous violence and heavy drinking habits, the magistrates' courts allowed him overnight access to Cheniel but refused him access to Ian. He collected Cheniel alternate weekends, Friday night until Sunday. Taking advantage of the situation, he began to verbally abuse me in front of my children, showing up when he felt like it and demanding certain rights, constantly bombarding me with uneasy questions and firing comments at me knowing that I couldn't defend myself in front of the children. Some Fridays we would be waiting around for hours and he wouldn't turn up at all.

I still lived local to him in a small council house in the middle of Staveley, but for some reason he thought I was an embarrassment to him and he would approach me in the streets arguing his rights and demand that I leave the area. He constantly pushed the fact that I didn't originate from there and considered me to be an outsider, different from anyone he knew. He hated the thought of me mixing with his friends and held me responsible for our break-up. I considered his demands to clear me out of town one of the best he had ever given me and approached the local council for a property exchange. I didn't really want to return to Chesterfield, but when the mutual exchange came through I grabbed it with both hands. It wasn't particularly the best move for me or my children but I knew I hadn't got much choice. So I accepted the large four bedroom house at Newbold, a fairly large estate on the outskirts of Chesterfield. It was quite a pleasant area close to my father's home so I didn't feel too isolated and Ian's new school was within walking distance, so I had no worries about getting him there. Nigel was right in a way, I didn't belong in Staveley but he was wrong about my origin. I had originated from that area, just a couple of miles up the road, but I had never trusted him enough to tell him everything about my abusive childhood or my upbringing. I had lost my broad Derbyshire accent and had learned to be more civilised so he didn't associate me with the local ruffians. Looking back I remember feeling a little insulted at the comments he had made about me being an outsider, but now I thank my lucky stars that I was different.

As far as I knew Arch still lived at Wingerworth and the house that I moved into was a few miles away from him on the other side of Chesterfield, so I had no worries about bumping in to him.

The children and I settled into our new home quite quickly and our lives began to improve. Ian made friends at school and Cheniel settled better than she ever had. It seemed with all the tension gone; she was content and grew beautifully. Then one day I was out shopping and bumped into Arch and his children; I suppose it was inevitable considering we both used the same supermarket. We spoke to each other, although I didn't get time to tell him that I had moved house or where I had moved to. Purely out of embarrassment we quickly exchanged telephone numbers and said goodbye. He hadn't told me that he had moved from Wingerworth but when he telephoned me that same evening, I was surprised when he explained that he had sold the house at Wingerworth and bought one that was situated on Princess Street at Newbold, close to the Catholic school which Adam and Nicola attended. I was taken aback as it now seemed that he lived just a stone's throw away from us. I wasn't sure how to respond and it was a few minutes before I was able to acknowledge his statement. Then I began to laugh as a smile spread over my face. As I spoke to him I could hear the uncertainty in his voice and I wanted to put him at ease. I laughed again and explained that he could have just popped over the road for a coffee and saved himself a phone call! At first he didn't understand what I was trying to say but when I told him I could almost see his front door from where I stood, I heard him swallow and his breathing seemed to get a little louder but when he realised what I had said he began to laugh too and spoke with so much pleasure in his voice; I just knew he had missed me.

I met him that same afternoon and enjoyed coffee at his house. I wasn't surprised when I realised my feelings hadn't changed towards him and I knew straight away that he was the man I should have married. I loved him and no matter how long I spent away from him, my feelings never changed. We spoke for hours about our past and the future and laughed about the mistakes we had made. Then he got all serious on me and spoke about our daughter. He asked her name and wanted to know all about her. For the first time ever I was able to tell him everything about her birth, what she had weighed and the colour of her hair at birth. I showed him photographs, which he studied hard before asking if he could have one to keep in his wallet, then he suggested that he should see her. I had no right to refuse him; I knew that. He was her father and had every right to have contact with her and I wanted that more than anything, but I was scared. I had hurt him and I knew he wouldn't commit himself unless he was one hundred per cent certain that I wasn't going to hurt him again. I could understand him wanting to see her and I would have let him, but I was too cautious. He said there was no doubt she was beautiful and complimented her beautiful blonde curls. I felt the barrier that he had placed before him as he took her from my arms, but I could see that she had already won his heart as a tear trickled from his eye. He smiled at her while he held her in his arms and shook his head from side to side for me to see. I had done them a great injustice. I knew at that moment we could never go back, he was too cautious and I too scared of the feelings I had for him. Apart from the love I felt for my children, I had never felt so much warmth and tenderness for another person. Just thinking about him overwhelmed me. When I was with him my emotions were so out of control that I knew if I went back to him I would in time lose the will to override it and in no time at all I would feel trapped again. I tried to understand my feelings and the way I felt but my mind was so mixed up I couldn't.

I was living my life around my children, trying to give them all that I had never had but I wasn't sure what it was that I had missed and it felt like I was just trying to build castles in the sky. Eventually we both accepted that it wasn't the time for us to be together and so we separated, kidding ourselves that the future might be different.

I cried for hours that night wondering when the years passed by, would I still feel the same? Twenty-four years down the line I sit alone and cry, realising all I have missed and knowing all the time that he was the man I should have married.

I saw him only twice after then, so he knew nothing about Nigel gaining custody of Cheniel. Once I began to suffer with seizures, I felt too ashamed to contact him as I always thought he would blame me for my own fate. Before I was diagnosed with epilepsy, Nigel jumped at the chance to take care of Cheniel and took the opportunity to fight for custody of her, knowing that I was too ill to oppose his actions. I will never forgive him for using my daughter to get back at me and I hope that one day he will find it in his heart to accept his wrong doing and somehow make it up to her.

Like so many mums going through strife and turmoil, I was branded an unfit mother until I was well enough to prove otherwise. By that time it was too late; I had lost six long years of my daughter's life and still hadn't got her back. I have wondered many times why this had to happen to me and my young family, but no amount of whys or wherefores explain to me why it took place. The only thing that I can think of is that it must have been my fate that my children had to suffer so much during the process.

I have never gotten over losing my daughter and I will never forget the pain that I felt when he walked away with her. Although she eventually made her way back to me, it was ten long years later when she was almost a woman. Although I loved her with all my heart, I still couldn't help thinking about the little girl he had taken away from me. It was strange how people thought that giving birth to twins compensated for losing her, but they were wrong; nothing ever compensated. The memories of her never left me. She was always the sweet little girl that I had let slip away and, no matter how many years passed by, she was still four years old crying the same tears she cried when I had to let her go. Even now, each time I look at her I see that same little girl crying the tears she has always cried. I have nothing to compare with the heartache that I felt when I lost her and I can only suppose that I would have felt similar pain had I let her go with Arch. But what grieves me the most is knowing that she lived most of her life with a man who tried his utmost to alienate her from me, knowing that his ways were not the right ways and the love he portrayed to her was not genuine; and all because he sought revenge.

CHAPTER 6

Forever Running

When I finally left Chesterfield I assumed my life could only get better. My brother, John, had been stalking me most of my life and pursued me relentlessly. He had already abused me when I was a small child so I knew the only way I could try and rid myself from him was if I moved away from there. My father had often risked his own safety to ward him off me, but John was persistent and often appeared on my doorstep usually forcing his way over the threshold, threatening me into watching while he masturbated in front of me. I remained terrified of him and when I gave birth to my children I feared for their lives as well as my own.

My mother often questioned him about his perversions but he was very sly and managed to deceive her, so I spent most of my life fleeing from one place to another, too frightened to remain in any one place for too long. And yet again I suffered in silence, praying that he would leave me in peace and at the same time desperately trying to protect my children. The constant fear I had of him contributed towards my breakdown yet I couldn't see it coming. I thought of all sorts of ways to try to avoid him and his perversion - alienating him, befriending him and even threatening him with the strength of the law, but even that didn't deter him. In spite of everything, he carried on until my life got so bad I figured the only way out was for me to keep on running.

I even remember threatening to tell his wife, Pat; this was the only time I actually saw fear in his eyes. Pat was a large robust woman who, during our first meeting, gave me the impression that she would not tolerate him messing around. On several occasions I witnessed her putting John in his place and I could tell by his response that she had more power over him than he was willing to admit. I also noticed that when they had previously visited Mother's house, he had been unusually quiet and kept control of his need to satisfy his unnatural desire of self-gratification. Never once had he dared to make suggestive remarks or expose himself to me as he had done at my house, so it didn't take me long to work out that the only time that I was safe was when I was with her. I used Pat for my own protection, feeling guilty that my friendship towards her was not based on her own attributes but for the safety of myself and my children.

I recall how I left my home each morning taking Ian to school, but keeping Cheniel by my side, hoping I was out of the area well before John arrived at our house. Then I made my way to their house and remained there with Pat until he was due to return home to her. It was a strategy that worked, although I found it difficult to manoeuvre my children around him, particularly when I had to collect Ian from school and keep our health appointments. In the evenings when I put them to bed, I found it easier to turn off the lights and leave our house in total darkness, pretending we were not at home when he called. I was always under the impression that Pat was never aware of anything and for some reason she accepted my coming and going as the norm. I wasn't the only member of my family to frequently visit her but, having noticed there was something not quite right between John and me, she often asked me why we didn't get on like the rest of the family. As he carefully worked out my strategy, my life became unbearable and, like so many times before, I searched all counties for another place to live, hoping that somehow I could avoid him. It was only during a visit to see my mother that I saw my younger sister, Lorraine, who informed me that there was a property to let next door to her. It was situated in Mansfield Woodhouse, in a less desirable area than I was used to, but needless to say I jumped at the chance of renting it and thanked my lucky stars that the landlord allowed me to move in almost immediately.

I thought moving next door to Lorraine was the kind of protection that I needed, although I felt really sad at the thought of leaving Newbold as I knew that my father would have to fend for himself again. He had gotten used to me doing his laundry and cooking his main meal. He had reached the age where he had found it difficult to cope with household chores and very often neglected himself, but there was no alternative. I had to think about myself and couldn't allow my father's care to jeopardise the safety of my children. It was at that point of my life that I began to think about all the lives that John had destroyed and I realised, no matter how many years had passed, he still continued to feed his addiction of self-gratification by abusing and raping those who couldn't defend themselves. I was just one of many who suffered from his vicious attacks and, because he had been committing offences of a similar nature for so long, he accepted it as the norm.

Father was angry when I told him I couldn't remain in Chesterfield and more so when I told him the reasons why. He approached my other brother, David, as he had done on many occasions just to let him know what John was doing to me and what I had to put up with. He sought David's help but he had already formed a close alliance with John, so anything that Father told him fell on deaf ears really. I recall having spoken to David once myself but John was far more deceitful and cunning than I, so could twist and turn a tale better than any fine author. So just like Mother, David was taken in by John's lies as he continued to abuse me; just as he always had.

I didn't want John to know that I was moving away from Chesterfield or where I was moving to, so my younger brother, Andrew, assisted my father in helping me to do a moonlight flit. It took only a few hours to pack our belongings. What I couldn't fit into Father's trailer, I left behind. Although I felt so relieved once I had left, I felt sad that I had to leave at all.

When I arrived in Mansfield Woodhouse, I noticed that there was a lot more to it than I had actually remembered. Although we travelled through some pleasant parts, I had forgotten what it was like in and around the less desirable areas. I could have cried a mountain of tears when Father pulled his car to a halt outside the front door of Number One Manvers Street. It was an old empty house with broken-down windows and looked as if it hadn't been occupied for years. I felt physically sick as I climbed out of the car and stepped onto the pavement and into a heap of stale vomit. At that precise moment I felt like turning around and going straight back again. I wasn't sure that I was doing the right thing staying but, because of the terrible anguish that John caused me, I was in no fit state to do anything else. I was so disappointed in the condition of the house and I felt so sorry for my children; they had never been used to living in filth and disarray and I wasn't sure that I knew how to put it all right for them. Father and Andrew helped me to unload my furniture and the children's toys and it seemed that in no time at all I was left sorting out the chaos so they could get back home and in bed before daybreak.

It took me close to three months to clean and decorate that house, and a few more weeks to furnish it. I was exhausted by the time it was finished and swore to myself that I would never allow John to force me into moving again.

I registered myself, Ian and Cheniel with a doctor at the local surgery and managed to get young Ian into school, and within six months I had met Paul Marshall, my future husband. The first thing I noticed about him was that he was very streetwise and had the ability to protect himself from the more unpleasant and violent characters that my children and I now had to live around. I had never felt safe but when I gave birth to Ian and Cheniel, I felt even more of a need of protection. Although I had always maintained that I would never marry for anything but love, I knew the instant that I met Paul I would marry him. He wasn't really my type; his manners were atrocious and he had a terrible reputation for brawling in the streets, which always resulted in the police arresting him. But I figured that if everything I had heard about him was true, then he was the perfect candidate to protect us from John. The news of us getting married soon travelled around and my family's curiosity began to unfold. After all, I was twenty-six years old and by their standards way past marrying age, so I suppose they wondered who it was that I was getting married to. My brother, David, was the first to show up at the house to congratulate me. I was out shopping at the time so he left a message with Paul's sister, Julie, who was babysitting. She was a little taken back by his size and described him as being a giant! I suppose, judging by the Marshalls' structure, he was but from the description that she gave to me, I felt sure that I didn't know anyone of that structure so assumed the caller was just a rather largely-built salesman. I wasn't unduly worried about the unknown caller as I hadn't told any of my family where I had moved to and, apart from Andrew, Lorraine and my parents, I assumed that no-one else knew where I lived. So the fear of John or any member of my family turning up on my doorstep was the furthest from my mind.

I recall it was 8pm by the time I had unpacked all the shopping and, just as I was putting the last few items into the freezer, I heard a rather loud knocking on my back door which instantly startled me. Immediately I felt apprehensive, as it was dark and the lamp above my back door had already been vandalised by the locals. It was quite isolated at the back of the house and my garden faced a plot of spare land that the locals used for dumping all their waste material at night. However my sister's Alsatian dog, Max, kept us pretty safe. He was always in her back yard and a quick call of his name would have brought him tumbling over our fence, so I wasn't as frightened as I had been in Chesterfield.

When I finally plucked up the courage to open the door, I was shocked to see David standing there. He had never been the type to come visiting, in fact I had only known him to do so on one other occasion when I lived in Chesterfield, so I couldn't help feeling concerned about his sudden appearance, especially at that time of night. Having asked him in I made us both a cup of coffee and tried to keep a conversation going until Paul came around. He always called to see me about 8pm, but for some reason that night he was a little late. When he did finally show, David revealed the reason why he had called. With his hand outstretched ready to shake Paul's hand, he remarked, 'So this is the man I've heard so much about. I hear you have a bit of a reputation.' Trying to remain calm, Paul shook David's hand firmly but unthreateningly and gave a rather noticeable 'urgh!' David smiled in an unintimidated way before loosening his grip and sitting down. I found the body language of both men quite interesting. Neither wanted to ruffle the other's feathers, but each wanted the other to know who the cock was! I could see by their expressions that they had a certain amount of respect for each other's firmness and strength but it was the long firm handshake and glare in their eyes that told me that they were wary of each other.

Once they had established the fact that they could be quite a match for each other, they drank their coffee and chatted about work and heavy trucks while I sat and weighed up the consequences if ever they were to fight. David stayed for a good two hours and talked about everything but the reason he called. He was friendly but evasive and, because I knew him, I was aware of his inquisitiveness about Paul. My family had never liked competition where strength was concerned and I felt that David was representing members of my family that I had not tolerated for some time. He had always been the most respected amongst us all, so I suppose he realised that I wouldn't turn him away from my door. I was only too pleased to introduce Paul to him. Although I knew David wouldn't be frightened of him, I just knew that once the rest my family was aware of him it would put some members on edge and certainly make my life a little more stable. After the longstanding abuse of me and my children, it seemed the only way out was to introduce a match to them. My family worked in very peculiar ways. One had to know them well to comprehend their actions and I knew them well enough to know that Paul represented a threat to them; I wasn't ashamed of that. For the first time in my life I felt confident that John would not be lurking around my home, peering through my windows, demanding his way in with the purpose of assaulting me. At the age of twenty-six it was the only time that I had felt really protected. Being able to walk down the street without the fear of being jumped upon and forcibly pulled into a bush was overwhelming. My life was so much better once I had realised that John was too frightened to come near me. Finally I felt safe, alive and free to go anywhere I pleased, without being stalked or raped! I married Paul soon after because of that.

When I was told by my GP that I was pregnant again, I panicked and couldn't for the life of me think how I would cope with another baby. Each time I had become pregnant my biggest worry was wondering how I would protect the child from my brother, John. I had tried every type of contraception trying to avoid pregnancy but the Pill made me violently sick and condoms proved to be so unreliable the only alternative was to be sterilised, which I eventually opted for. I knew it wasn't safe for me to bring any more children into the world while John was alive, as there was always a possibility that he might hurt one of them too. So, in kindness to the children I decided that it would be my last pregnancy. What I hadn't anticipated was conceiving twins! As far as we were aware, neither Paul nor I had a history of twins in the family so I couldn't believe what was happening to me. It took me some time to convince myself that having one more child wouldn't make such a difference to our family circumstances, but when I had my first scan and realised that I was expecting twins I was mystified and felt sure I wouldn't cope. As always, I hid away my fears and self-doubts and when they arrived I celebrated the birth of our much-loved babies, Kyle and Allishia. They were born two weeks premature on February 2nd 1987 and weighed a healthy 6lb 2oz and 6lb 6oz. I was told it was unusual for twins to be born so large, but I suppose it was inevitable considering the structure of our families. I can't deny that I found them hard work, despite the midwife's recommendations of enjoying them while they were young.

Unfortunately Paul suffered from grand mal epilepsy and added to my worries and my workload, so my nervous disposition soon began to show and within no time at all I became ill again. I began to suffer from panic attacks and found myself so ill I couldn't even cope with everyday chores. I didn't find life easy being married to Paul; the constant hassle he caused, the police, court dates and appearances soon got me down. It was something I hadn't considered before marrying him and after a short while I began to regret ever marrying him at all. It didn't take me long to realise that it would take a much stronger person than I to live with him. I was constantly reminded of the differences between us and often received comments from our local police officers who frequently arrested him. I tried to keep him out of trouble and put everything I had into making our marriage work, but he was so exhausting that eventually I found no pleasure in being with him. Every time I thought we were doing okay he would get himself arrested and I would spend night after night all alone in the house, taking care of the children.

In time I began to miss Arch and our intellectual conversations and felt my life was just wasting away, so I thoughtlessly engaged in an affair with a police officer named Terry who had once arrested Paul. At first I felt terribly guilty about it, but Terry had this natural ability to put my mind at rest and helped me to realise that the kind of life I was living was not a good life for me or the children. He spoke a lot about living a normal life and enjoying it, which of course I knew nothing about! My life had always been disparate so I had no idea what I should expect or how to turn things around, but in time he helped me to achieve a better standard of living although in turn he used me for the more sordid side of things. I didn't feel I was cheating on Paul; I was merely living by his rules. He had had so many affairs in the short time we had been married that I could barely keep count of them. Because he was slightly younger than me, I had convinced myself that he needed to spread his wings now and again.

For reasons I don't fully understand I had always felt that it was a man's prerogative to find some unsuspecting woman to satisfy his sexual appetites. Although I found it difficult to accept that Paul didn't really care about me, in time I learned to turn a blind eye to his escapades and hoped that his attraction to other women would subside and that he would eventually settle down; but he never did.

My affair with Terry lasted all the way through my and Paul's legal separation and onset of divorce. Then I realised that even that relationship wasn't going anywhere, so I ended that too. It had been a pleasant affair and I never had any regrets. Somehow it proved to be a blessing in disguise, as I am sure had it not been for him I would never have had the strength to divorce Paul or even to face up to reality. I suppose in my own way I loved him, but there had been so many things go wrong with the relationships I had previously had that I felt no desire to put things right.

I had so little faith in men; it was just unfortunate that I never had enough trust in any of them to work things out. As soon as things began to go wrong I walked away, hurt but still in control. Although I had spent most of my life answering to other people, I felt at that point of my life that their worth did not enter into the equation and I gave consideration only to my children. Had it not been for them, I would no longer be a part of this world.

I recall that as being one of the most devastating times of my life. I hadn't been well for some time and the constant worry once again triggered anxiety depression. All I thought about was the rotten life that I had had and the guilt that I felt for not providing my children with anything better. My brother, John, had once again hunted me down and began calling at our house, so before I knew it my circumstances were exactly the same as they had been a couple of years before, when I had moved away from Chesterfield. No doubt he was out of control and pestered me unremittingly. The very thought of him touching my children horrified me. It had been a few years since I had seen him and the shock of seeing him again literally struck me with panic and sent me soaring over the top. Without any prior warning I suffered my first seizure, which automatically triggered severe anxiety attacks and caused me all kinds of terrifying symptoms. I became so ill that I was unable to care for myself or my children. But when I finally approached Mansfield Social Services to ask for their help, they were convinced that I didn't need it so I was just left to suffer in silence - the way I always had.

In time my body and mind broke down completely and I begged my sister, Carol, to accompany me to the hospital, but doctors didn't seem to recognise my symptoms and I was dismissed with all kinds of diagnostic excuses. I was given tape recordings of trees and branches swaying in the wind, rivers and brooks rippling over stones and the sounds of birds chorusing the dawn, but as peaceful as it sounds it didn't cure my seizures. Time seemed to drift by slowly while I suffered in so much pain. The strange sensations inside my head seemed to control every movement that I made and affected every little thing that I did, until eventually I was unable to speak without dribbling saliva or slurring my words. My bodily functions had slowed down and I became worn and pale, trembling from head to foot. I couldn't sleep and it seemed that I had been battling with it for so long that the thought of dying became a welcoming thought. Eventually I lost the will to live.

On that day I gave up my lifelong struggle of trying to protect myself from John and finally accepted defeat. I placed my children with those I thought more capable of taking care of them and abandoned all our belongings and family home, then simply waited for the inevitable to happen. It was by sheer coincidence that my sister, Julia, and her husband, Chris, had stopped travelling and had decided to visit me only to find me so distraught and ill with worry that I couldn't stop myself crying long enough to tell them what was wrong. I hadn't seen them for some time and yet they offered me and Ian a home, knowing that I wasn't well enough to take care of myself, or Ian. He was the only child that remained with me. I sobbed uncontrollably as I realised that after all the years of running and hiding, not only had I allowed John to ruin my life but my children's lives as well.

I had always felt ashamed of being mauled and sexually abused by him and for some reason I had always blamed myself for being born into the same family. I was always frightened of the things that he said and did to me and, although I was no longer a child, I was even more frightened of him. As a young teenager I had learned to hide the fact that I had been sexually abused by him, as I had become aware that not everyone understood about such things and many tended to think that I was equally to blame for it. It seemed that being a teenager I was expected to have enough brawn to ward off any assailants without complaining about it. I was constantly reminded by certain members of my family that John was my brother and, for reasons I will never be able to understand, I wasn't expected to condemn him for what he had done. Instead, I was expected to trust and respect him; my duty for being his sister. Yet no-one expected him to have the same loyalty or respect for me. This was something I had grown up with, so never once questioned it - not even to myself. I suppose my brain had been implanted with so many wrong ideas of sexual abuse that I found it difficult to accept that I was the innocent one.

The last thing I remember doing before leaving our family home was desperately trying to pack as many items of clothing and photographs of my children into black bags, and wondering how the hell I was going to fit Cheniel's large dolls' house that she loved so much into a small space in the back of the car which I could barely fit myself into.

Suddenly my mind goes blank; no memories or happy thoughts of my children growing up; no heartache or suffering; just a total blank; months of family life forgotten.

Julie and Chris were a Godsend. They helped me to pick up the pieces and cared for my son while I battled with undiagnosed epilepsy and severe anxiety depression. Then together we fought long and hard for the return of my other children, Cheniel, Kyle and Allishia. I was labelled an unfit mother and called names by authoritative individuals who had lived normal lives, but who failed to understand that there were still many of us who hadn't. It was obvious to me that they found it easier to identify my mistakes than to comprehend that all of that ruin was the typical aftermath of child abuse.

—⟋⟍—

CHAPTER 7

Trying to Build a New Life

After months of convalescing, I applied to East Lindsey District Council for a three bedroom council house in Old Bolingbroke, a tiny rural village on the outskirts of Lincoln. Hoping to turn my life around, I fought for a tenancy that I wasn't really entitled to, in an area I didn't really want to live in. But desperation conquered all and within no time at all I had moved into Old Bolingbroke, hoping it would give me the opportunity to provide stability for my children and a chance to obtain custody of all three of them.

For two long years I felt desperately homesick. On occasions I travelled to Chesterfield just to give myself that sense of belonging and yet, when I arrived there, all the memories of the fear and panic that I felt when I was a small child came flooding back, reminding me of everything I needed to escape from. My desire to run and hide influenced my return to Old Bolingbroke but things didn't go too well for me or my children. Being a single mother I was instantly frowned upon and discussed by many of the locals, who at times were rude and insensitive, so I became lonely and very unhappy. Admittedly I was still very reserved and spoke with a slightly different accent to the locals, but until I met

Norma Down I hadn't realised how much my own demeanour affected the amount of people that spoke to me. The majority of local women were somewhat unsociable and I was unusually timid, so I found it almost impossible to converse with them. Norma, on the other hand, was bright and cheerful. Coming from Stockton-on-Tees, she was extremely extrovert and delightfully approachable so it seemed we got on well with each other. Her flirtatious manner reminded me of my old school friend, Marie Butler… I was just a child then and lived at the Outrake Children's Home. The swirling poses Norma created with her bright floral sun dresses bought happy memories flooding back of Marie dancing proudly in the street wearing my bright yellow party dress that she claimed as her own for a while. If I hadn't known better, I would have sworn that Marie and Norma were the same two people; they were so alike it was uncanny, so it took me no time at all to make Norma my friend. Apart from her distinctive dress sense, she was gracious and forthcoming. Although I got the impression that she liked to think herself hard-hearted and uncharitable, she was in fact generous to a fault. In all the years that I knew her, she never saw me or my children go without. When I fell upon hard times and struggled to feed them, she was always there for me and offered help without making me feel demoralized or guilty. The years between us were very few but in general she seemed much older than me, so I always liked to think that I gave her the respect that she deserved. I had known her for several years before I eventually confided in her. I had always tried to hide the fact that I was ill, that way I didn't really have to explain something that I didn't understand. But occasionally I would have a recurrence of seizures and panic attacks, so eventually I found it easier to confide in her rather than allow her to think that I was just going crazy. She didn't seem to pity me and, although I felt sure that she was shocked at some of the things I told her about, she seemed to pass them off as if they were nothing and as always repeated her favourite quotation, 'never mind, worse things happened at sea.' I was pleased that she took that attitude; in a strange kind of way it helped me to remain calm during a time of anxiousness. There were times when she gave me the impression that she knew all about epilepsy by saying, 'You're really lucky that you don't suffer from grand mal epilepsy, like Brian.' It was only years later that I appreciated what she had been trying to do and realised that she held very little knowledge of the disease and hadn't got a clue which type, if any, was better to suffer from. Then one day she confessed to me that she was terrified of my condition, for which I had to laugh as it had always been a disease I had feared too. So I understood where she was coming from.

Ever since I was a small child, I had been frightened of things that I hadn't been able to understand; epilepsy was just one of them. I wasn't really sure why. Before I went into the care homes I can't ever remember meeting anyone who suffered from it, although it seemed that I had been made aware of its debilitating factors well before then. Admittedly each time I had witnessed my husband, Paul, suffering a grand mal attack, I froze with fear. But even then I hadn't realised how painful seizures were until I suffered from them myself. Then I understood only too well how horrific and undignified they could be. Although I was never able to understand why I began to suffer from them, the fact that I did always worried me. It wasn't something I could run or hide from and the thought of having to put up with them for the rest of my life was absolutely daunting. I found it almost impossible to remember anything that was so painful. Even with medication, I suffered from prolonged symptoms that interfered with my faculties and caused me so much pain and uncertainty that I often wished I hadn't been born at all.

The twins had been in care for almost eighteen months before I was eventually allowed them home. They had grown and were happy to be at home and I was overjoyed to have them, but I wasn't one of those mothers who viewed situations through rose-coloured spectacles and I could see that my babies had changed. I suppose in a way I had too, but I tried to pick up where I had left off. I hadn't planned on running into difficulties as I, like many other mothers, allowed my heart to rule my head and although I tried so hard not to let it, I didn't give myself time to consider what 'being in care' may have done to them. I had already been made aware that since my breakdown, they had been moved from pillar to post, in and out of foster homes around Mansfield County. This added to their insecurities and caused them to suffer emotionally. It was almost impossible to get to the bottom of their behavioural problems. I had slight recollection of Rachel Carter, their social worker, who had previously informed me of the problems each foster parent encountered as they tried to cope with my hyperactive twins. But I couldn't recall her saying anything about them suffering through it. I suppose I should have had a little more insight, but I had heard so many people say that being in care was different now that I had rather expected them to come through it unscathed. What a fool I was to think that my children could have been parted from me without feeling abandoned and unsafe. I had been raised with lots of children who, like me, had been parted from their parents, but it seemed over the years I had forgotten just how desperate we all were to get back to them.

All my life I had been trying to make amends for something that wasn't my fault. When I came out of care I was fourteen years old and all I wanted to do was make good with my life. The only thing that I ever wished for was simplicity, but there I was with a life more complex than anything I had ever known.

Because I'd had so many unpleasant experiences as a child, I suffered continually from mental and emotional problems and because of that my children suffered too. I had tried so many times to turn my life around, but I found that if it wasn't my brother, John, taunting me, then it was my own state of mind that hindered my progress.

When I was young I had always assumed that my poor health and state of mind was solely the result of the abuse and neglect that I had suffered as a young child, but now I realise that it wasn't only down to that, but also a contribution of regular demands that some members of the Wass family made of me - just one more reason why I found Old Bolingbroke the ideal place to live. It was quiet and sedate and, although it was beautiful, it had up to that point managed to resist the seduction of mass tourism. And, above all else, my family were oblivious to its existence. I spent the first couple of years in Old Bolingbroke trying to make ends meet.

I continued the heartrending fight to have Cheniel returned to me but it never seemed to go the way I had hoped. I travelled to and from Chesterfield every other week to ensure that I kept regular contact with her and desperately tried to keep the bond between the four of my children alive, but even that proved difficult at times. I managed to enrol Ian into Spilsby High School, only to find that he was constantly bullied for his pleasant attributes, and then I began to wonder if I had done the right thing at all. I had spent twelve years caring for him, correcting his speech and teaching him good manners, for which I felt proud. Then I had to watch him suffer at the hands of children who hadn't been taught well at all. I cried on the nights that I wrote letters to his headmaster and again when I visited the school to complain. But nothing I said or did seemed to cure the problem of children bullying, so for years Ian remained an outsider. Each day he faced the gruelling task of attending school, knowing that he was going to be set upon. I witnessed him shed the same tears every morning and last thing at night, asking me the same old question. 'Why do the children pick on me, Mummy? Just one more question I couldn't answer. He was clean and well cared for, affectionate and good-hearted and yet he suffered terribly. Each year he received a fine report from each teacher and won the Pupil of the Year award... so little recognition for the price he had to pay. Of course I blamed myself. Although I spent years going over my own upbringing, trying to decipher the good from the bad so that I could teach my children right from wrong, it seemed that no matter what I did I got it wrong anyway and my children paid the price. Ian was almost fourteen by the time I was well enough to protect him and by that time he had grown so used to the kind of violence he met within the school that nothing seemed to worry him.

Looking back I was lucky when I met Brian, Pat and their three girls, Julie, Leanne and Michelle. Their genuine concern and goodwill gave us a lifeline to cling to - something we desperately needed. But their friendship gave us much more than I had ever hoped for. Julie was a pretty sixth form student, wild and free, yet she put a wing around Ian in a bid to protect him from her unruly class mates. She set up a free-for-all arm wrestling competition purposely for young Ian to display his party piece. Fortunately for him my ex-husband, Paul, had shown him the technique of winning every game of arm wrestling without the need for strength to do it. Knowing that it took brains, not brawn, won Ian the respect of every sixth form student that day and finally, after suffering four long years of fear and torment, he came home smiling. When he and Julie arrived home that day our house was in total uproar and even more so when Julie puckered her lips and gave him his very first kiss.

Ian remained at Spilsby High School, setting an example for other children to follow, and finished his last day smothered in eggs and flour just like every other student who had reached the tender age of sixteen. For the very last time I stood and watched him as he got off the school bus, with his hands tucked into his pockets and his rucksack on his back, dribbling and kicking the same tatty old football down Hagnaby Road that he had been kicking ever since we had arrived there. It felt strange watching him approach the house knowing that it would be the last time that he would accompany the twins off the school bus and down the road, and just for a split second I recalled his very first day at school and wept for a while. Time had passed so quickly and yet I had found it so hard to grasp at life sometimes; it seemed that memories were all I had left. In sixteen years I had come so far and yet my children were my only treasures. All I ever wanted to do was make them happy.

Old Bolingbroke eventually grew on us all and in time we made the village our home and our house our castle. I gradually got to know everyone and became part of the community. The twins, however, experienced lots of problems and found it a little more difficult. Eventually they made friends with Norma's' son, Christopher, who was three years older than them but he was so small he made a good friend for them. He appeared problematic and experienced difficulty coping with everyday tasks, but he learned to use the twins to stimulate his memory, making things a little easier for himself. Although I had experienced my fair share of problems with the twins, I felt sorry for Norma. Before Christopher was diagnosed with a short memory span, she worried continually at the thought of him not being able to read and write at the same pace as other children and became embarrassed when he showed no interest in reciting his ABC's like the twins did. He failed to make progress at school and showed very little interest academically. It was only then that I realised how advanced the twins really were in comparison to him. Then she asked me to help her. It was an unusual situation really. I had always known Norma to be independent, but even so I felt quite proud to be able to return one small favour for all the favours she had done for me in the past. After putting the twins into bed, I spent hours every night trying to teach Christopher how to spell his name, until I noticed that the biggest problem that he had was remembering which letter his name began with. It was difficult not to jump to conclusions and I felt sad that I eventually had to. Christopher was almost eight years old and, because of Norma's embarrassment, he had suffered all kinds of ridicule from the children for something that wasn't his fault. It was one of the saddest situations I had ever come across. Although she was a very loving and proud mother, Norma tried to hide Christopher's problems hoping that he would grow out of them but he was the talk of Old Bolingbroke well before Norma decided to confide in me. Although I had thought long and hard about approaching her before then, I knew she wouldn't have thanked me for it. It felt good being in the right place at the right time. For the first time in years I was able to help someone without being manipulated into it. Although I had never been taught the importance of caring, it seemed to be an instinct that I was born with and I found it pleasing to help her.

Life in Old Bolingbroke wasn't so bad. Despite my ill health and inhibitions, I was finally accepted for the person I was and gradually made friends with the majority of my neighbours. I was able to confide in one or two of them and in return they trusted me. It was extremely quiet there, reminding me of my childhood days at Monsal Dale. Although I had lived in so many different parts of the country, I found that I remembered Monsal Dale with such clarity; a place that once held me captive now haunted me with its unforgettable beauty. I remembered the brief moments of happiness that I had there and, despite the miles between Monsal Dale and Old Bolingbroke, it seemed that I still held the memories of Monsal Dale closest to my heart. I gave very little thought to the towns I had once lived in and became so accustomed to Old Bolingbroke that I never expected to leave.

Understanding very little about the symptoms of epilepsy, I struggled with intermittent paralysis of the limbs and over the years experienced many problems regarding my health, but the relaxed life style of the village helped me to keep my life at a steady pace and under control. I had previously undergone several operations so found it difficult to come to terms with a disability that I wasn't born with, but nevertheless I persevered and took care of my children the best way I could.

The twins' social worker, Peggy Clapham, called once in a while for a quick chat and a pat on the back for co-operating with her, but nothing more than that.

Despite having faith, it was difficult to carry on with life in a normal way. Had it not been for young Ian, I and my young family would never have survived. Sometimes I felt so low I cried until my head hurt but I kept on gruelling, hoping that everything would turn out fine. Every night I prayed, asking God to forgive me for letting my children down and begged him to allow Cheniel the freedom of choice. Lying awake at night, I recited the only prayer I could remember. Beginning with 'Our Father' I repeated The Lord's Prayer over and over again until I felt so choked I could barely swallow. Finding every day a challenge, I sometimes wished my children's lives away. Raising them hadn't proved to be the happy time I had dreamed about and the life I afforded them didn't correspond with the hopes and dreams I had once planned out for them. Many times I had wondered if I was doing as well as my own mother had done for me. When my thoughts were unclear, I sometimes asked myself if they might have been better off without me. Drifting in and out of the anomalous world I felt so safe in, I recalled the cold and lonely nights where I had lain in my bed as a child, fearful of the sexual abuse that almost crippled me, and I asked myself: Who am I? Am I who I should be?

—m—

CHAPTER 8

My Life's Long Journey

It always created excitement when a new face arrived in Old Bolingbroke and there was no exception when Brian's brother, Eddie, arrived from Colchester. The state of his marriage and the reason for its breakdown was put about well before his arrival, and anyone who knew him sympathized with him. Although I had heard slightly conflicting stories, it seemed that he'd had a rough time of it and the story he repeatedly told of his estranged wife, Sue, hurling vinegar into his face seemed to continually circulate the village, discrediting her name. Eddie and Sue had suffered six turbulent years of rows and reconciliations and it seemed at that point their relationship had hit rock bottom and there was no turning back. It was difficult for me to feel sorry for a man in his position and I found myself wondering about the woman who everyone seemed to have turned against; my heart seemed to lie with her. Although I didn't know her, I knew only too well what she was going through. I first met Eddie when I had been invited to Brian and Pat's for coffee. It was usual for me to join their house load of guests at night; living next door it was convenient for me and I must admit I found it pretty good fun. But the night I met Eddie I felt a little apprehensive. Knowing his circumstances, I felt a little embarrassed but I gritted my teeth and made my way round to the house, hoping I wouldn't panic and change my mind at the last minute. Before I knew it I had reached their front door and been invited inside, where I was introduced to Eddie. I felt very uncomfortable and stood in silence for a while. Having heard so much gossip about him, I had expected him to be short and stocky and a little surly like his brother, but he wasn't like that at all. In fact he was quite the opposite. Although I didn't find him handsome, occasionally I would glance across at him and realise that his overall appearance provoked a desirable response within me. He was tall, slim and every ounce a gentleman. Although I found his sense of humour a little outrageous, his manners were impeccable so I couldn't help but like him. We spoke very little and, apart from the occasional glance, I kept well clear of him for fear my vibes would be sensed by others.

Having lived in Old Bolingbroke for quite a while I had got to know Brian pretty well. Suffering from epilepsy, we shared a lot of the same fears and empathized with each other. Although our relationship was purely platonic, it proved to be one of the most sincere relationships that I had ever experienced; there was no pretence or deceit and we found that we could always be honest and frank without thinking any less of each other. I couldn't ever remember hurting his feelings and I knew that he would never have intentionally hurt mine. When I first met him he showed me that he was no pushover. Despite his harelip and slight facial disfigurement, he had enough confidence to ask me to sleep with him but on both occasions I subtly let him down, knowing that my rejections wouldn't come between us. Many nights we rolled around with laughter after telling each other jokes then spent hours smoking heavily and sipping warmed brandy, telling each other untold secrets and honouring ourselves for our previously wicked ways. It seemed there was nothing we couldn't talk about but then I began to pick up on the local gossip, which caused me to feel a little uncomfortable spending so much time alone with him. I became very cynical and began to doubt his intentions and searched my mind for reasons why I should remain such good friends with him. Our friendship slowly faded and Brian became a little distant. Although we still occasionally saw each other, we seemed to go our own way and things never seemed to be the same again. I still went round to their house for coffee and occasionally he came to mine, but from that time on he always seemed moody and snapped at everything I said.

I never stopped visiting Brian, although it seemed easier when Pat was there, so I generally went round at weekends when I knew that he was out socializing. Then one day I decided to go round during the day and found that the only person there was Eddie. Although he asked me inside, I felt dubious about staying and felt myself tremble at the thought of being alone with him. Yet the very thought of being lured into a situation I couldn't drag myself away from really excited me. Although I was aware that there would be no turning back, I accepted an invitation to go in and sit down without giving it too much thought. I didn't want to give him the impression that I was frightened of being alone with him, but I didn't want to portray that I was in desperate need of company either. He offered to make me a cup of coffee and I sat down on the sofa watching every move that he made through the old bevelled-edged mirror that hung on the wall just above the fireplace in front of me. And, just as before, I began to feel the same urge of desire that I felt when I had first met him. Although I couldn't understand what it was about him that appealed to me, my instincts told me that he was feeling exactly the same way. Being rather reserved I didn't have the nerve to approach him, so I tried to think of ways to let him know how I was feeling without giving him the impression that I was in desperate need of sexual gratification. I didn't want to appear unapproachable, although I was aware that I sometimes surrounded myself with a protective barrier so solid that men usually stayed pretty clear of me. I had never been an easy person to approach and for obvious reasons I occasionally gave out strong vibes of disgust in the presence of men, so I knew I had to try really hard to control my imperviousness if I wanted him to make an advance towards me. I was really cautious of making an advance towards him as I had always been terrified of being rejected.

I had been known to flirt but I was a little wary of Eddie. His mind seemed to be anywhere but with me and the topic of his conversations was always Sue and their kids. I watched through the mirror as he carefully carried two hot cups of coffee from the kitchen to the lounge, totally unprepared for what he had to say to me. I listened with disbelief as he blatantly accused me of having an affair with his brother. Lost for words, I sat back in disgust. I couldn't believe he was so stupid! I was so sure that I had given out the right signals but it was obvious at that point that he thought that my interest lay with Brian. I must admit I was a little taken aback and became very angry at the thought of being accused of something I hadn't done. I sat forward in my seat and contemplated leaving well before I gave myself time to think over what he had said. My natural instincts were to try and plead my innocence but I was reluctant to speak to him. Feeling ashamed and totally embarrassed, I got up to walk out. I didn't know him so I didn't feel that I owed him an explanation. He didn't respond to my disgruntled movements until I got up to leave then, seemingly as an afterthought, he jumped to his feet and guarded the door as I approached him. Taking a deep breath I firmly gripped the door handle, trying my damnedest to pull open the door, but found that the grip he had with one hand was far sturdier than the grip I had with two. At that moment I realised I had come face-to-face with a similar situation that I remembered only too well from my past. Hating the very thought of being restrained, I became so frightened and distressed that my heart began to race and I became hysterical. Sweat ran from my brow as I began to panic and suddenly the fear of hyperventilating again caused me to break down. I stood in front of him, trembling as I readily accepted defeat. Fearing only the worst, I mumbled how much I hated men like him.

It seemed that many things frightened me, but nothing more than the circumstances I was in at that moment. Being alone with a man who wilfully overpowered me left me feeling so vulnerable that my mind drifted back to my childhood days, where I was the horrified victim of child abuse. I didn't need to associate myself with men, but somehow it seemed that I always got myself caught up in fatalistic events that determined my future. I could see by Eddie's expression that he was flummoxed by my weak side and just for a moment he took a long hard look at me, taking stock of all the unpleasant changes to my personality. He waited for me to calm down before he gently wrapped his arms around me and delivered me a kiss that was so intense and passionate; I was instantly aroused by it. The very instant his lips met mine I felt my knees buckle as the thought of sleeping with him entered my mind. Taking a single step forward, I manoeuvred the whole of my body towards his. Having almost tasted the sensuous aroma of his cologne, I could scarcely deny myself the pleasure of him comforting me. He spoke words of comfort that were particularly soft and caring and, despite my uncontrolled outburst, I found myself responding to his delicate touch. While I could not imagine what we were about to encounter, I allowed him to lovingly embrace me as he gently lowered me to the floor. I had never made love so impulsively but found his uncontrolled trembling at the point of no return so exciting. Making love to him was incredible. Although I had promised myself that I would never get involved with a man again, I found him irresistible; the force between us felt so overwhelming I lost all my inhibitions and journeyed twice.

After that night, Eddie and I became really close. I listened whilst he compared me to the women he had known previously and found the stories of sex within his marriage far more exciting than I should have done, but it seemed to work well for both of us. I didn't react like most women so he tended to confess more and more about his life with his wife and even told me about them taking part in wife-swapping. I wasn't really sure whether he was just teasing me or trying to shock the hell out of me, but I listened intensely without raising an eyebrow or passing comment. The whole idea of sleeping with someone else's partner while mine slept with theirs didn't appeal to me, but when he introduced me to a couple he had once been involved with I almost changed my mind. I wasn't sure if it was the unknown that made the offer seem so appealing or the fact that the whole idea was so taboo. Even so, after being genuinely coaxed and ladled with alcohol, I couldn't bring myself to make love to another man who solely wanted me for his own pleasure. I wasn't quite as daring as I thought I might have been. I couldn't see myself sitting in a large comfy chair in someone else's home while Eddie indulged in casual sex with another woman, although I must admit I didn't find any of it repulsive or indeed beyond my own imagination. And at times I tried so hard to overcome my inner fear so that I could taste a little of what seemed so exciting.

When I got to know Eddie better, I realised that we were far more compatible than I originally thought and, despite his genuine attraction to other women, I found that he was honest about it and I trusted him. Within that first year I tried to convince him that I was the woman he had been searching for all his life. Initially behaving like an innocent child, I was pleasantly naive and simply gullible. Progressing to an over-excited female with slight sophistication, I gradually built up an excessive balance of sexual desire, willing only to please the man I was falling in love with, but in time I began to wonder if we were allowing our sex lives to become the most important thing in our lives. As the increased pleasure of the flesh gradually took precedence over everything else, it left me feeling sad and empty. My need to be loved by him was so high I was almost willing to give up everything to remain in his favour. Then one day I realised that I was trying so hard to compete with the women he had been involved with, that I almost fell apart at the thought of losing him. I dedicated every minute of every day to him hoping that I would be more than just a shadow of their existence, but I knew he couldn't settle. He thought nothing of returning to Colchester for overnight stays and long weekends and I was oblivious to the fact that his ex-wife returned to Old Bolingbroke on odd occasions to be near him. I realised only too well that I was allowing myself to be caught up in one of Old Bolingbroke's 'old marriage stake-outs' but I continued to walk around with my eyes closed, allowing the only time I had on this earth to pass me by.

Enjoying what seemed to be the only pleasure I deserved, I watched the suns rise and evenings fall, wishing silently for a little happiness to come my way. I became old and decrepit-looking. Smothered in a protective balm, I forgot everything that I had ever wished for and clearly accepted that there was nothing more to life than that. But then I received my wake-up call on the morning I lost my father. I was devastated by the news of his death. Although I always expected him to die much before I was aged thirty, I had been spared the terrible heartache for just a few more years. Then I cried a mountain of tears that trickled down my face, seemingly cleansing away a multitude of sins that I had unpurposely gathered on my life's long journey; and there I was ready to begin again. The last few words that my father spoke rang repeatedly through my mind and the will of his spirit passed through me. For the first time in months I felt the warmth of his presence at the side of me. Guiding me, he helped me to make decisions that I was once incapable of making. Strange as it seemed, it was the things that I had never believed in that gave me the strength to carry on and, for reasons unknown to me, I felt that he was responsible for that. Suddenly I felt so strong and looked forward to the future, knowing there was nothing out there to harm me. I tried to bury the past and build my life around Eddie, the children and the little house and garden that my father loved so much. Feeling really appreciative of the short time that he had spent there, I thanked God for allowing him that little extra time so that he could appreciate the beauty of Old Bolingbroke.

My life with Eddie seemed to get much better once he had decided to move in with me. I put aside all the negative thoughts and feelings that had been festering inside of me and began to think more positively. The thought of my life not turning out the way I had hoped had suddenly been erased from my mind and happiness seemed to spread throughout my home like strawberries and wine. After all my years of sadness and regret, I finally felt that the life I had always longed for was finally upon us. I was happy and content. Apart from my little girl, Cheniel, I could think of nothing more that I wanted. My children's birthdays seemed to come and go and our well planned Christmases were the highlight of the year. And I threw another big party at the end of each year just to remind us that there was another year to look forward too.

I always tried to start the New Year with a clean slate; whatever I was doing I tried to lay a path to a new foundation. I made plans for the future and caught up with any correspondence that had piled up during the festive season. Just like everyone, I made New Year's resolutions - only to break them a few weeks later. Some years I kept them longer than others but only when I was desperately trying to fit into other people's regimes. But nature seemed to have a way of turning things around to suit it, and I would fit right into whatever felt natural at the time. I never liked January much, it was cold and bleak, a depressive month with long drawn out nights and darkened skies. I was always ready for the first show of spring and looked forward to waking up to a brighter dawn. The cry of the newborn lambs echoed throughout the whole of Old Bolingbroke and my children seemed to display a sadness I couldn't relieve them of. As a parent, I desperately tried to keep them happy and hoped that they would look back on their childhood with favour. Although I hadn't made their lives easy, I hoped the good times that I created would exceed the bad, although at times I was sceptical.

—ᗰᗰ—

CHAPTER 9

Fighting a Losing Battle

My diary for the New Year always included court dates. I attended Barristers' and solicitors' appointments desperately seeking all the help that I could, hoping to find a new approach in which to bring Cheniel home. I knew the day would come when I would be free to express my concerns about Nigel taking care of her, but I had no idea it would take so long. I fought for seven long years, desperate to meet the Judge who was willing to sit and listen to my side of the story, hoping he would take note of all the deceit that had been used against me. It seemed to take all the time in the world to convince the courts that I was trustworthy, and the passing of the years saw Cheniel grow and I lost track of normal family life. I offered my children only half-measures of the love and affection that I felt for them, simply because I had become too frightened to love them more. Something happened to me when Cheniel was taken away. I knew I had more to give, but sharing my love equally between the three children I had at home and the little one that I had lost didn't seem to work somehow. My mind was constantly fixed on her name and I felt every ounce of heartache that surrounded her. Within time her absence from home damaged us all and slowly turned each one of us into an emotional cripple. For years I lay awake at night, hoping and praying that one day Nigel would see the light and bring her home knowing it was what she really wanted, but he was scorned and felt a desperate need to avenge me so kept her as his pawn.

At this stage I find it very difficult to record all the memories that have haunted me through my life. The heartache that once made me feel unworthy of the little lives that I had been entrusted with still gives me great pain and I find it almost impossible to recall every little detail with clarity or understanding. At this point I now realise I am unable to record every part of my life without hurting the ones I most love, although I feel an overwhelming power to let the world know who wronged me and why. I feel a much stronger desire to protect my children from the aftermath of past destruction.

Despite her continuous pleas, Cheniel was never allowed home. She lived in constant fear of hurting either one of us and for a while we all forgot that she was just a small child. It was difficult to remember that at the time, and allowing the responsibility to fall on her young shoulders should have made her hate both of us. It wasn't until she had reached her teenage years that I realised that if we didn't learn to give her more than we took from her, then we would lose her for good. I recognised the respect she held for Elaine, her substitute mother. Although I had my grievances, in time I learned to respect her too. She had been there for Cheniel and, although I was envious of that, I realised Cheniel may not have pulled through had it not been for her.

On my last day in court I was finally given the opportunity to speak out. My medication had begun taking effect, my epilepsy was almost under control, the panic attacks were few and far between and my speech had returned to normal. Once again I was treated with respect and everyone remembered that I was human too. I was given my final chance to speak openly about my reasons for placing Cheniel under the care of Nigel Hadfield and why it had taken me so long to gain the trust of the courts. On that day I was pardoned by the Judge and the books began to turn; for the first time in seven years, my word was worthy. The Judge believed me but only because I was prepared to once again have my name dragged through the court, knowing that it wasn't going to change the decision that he had already made; to leave my daughter with the man he branded a 'deceitful liar'. A man who had committed perjury, not once but many times knowing that I was too ill to prove a thing. Yet when the truth finally came out, the Judge still wouldn't allow me to take Cheniel home.

When the Judge finally closed the case, I was forced to accept that there was nothing more that I could do to bring her home and I began to focus on the twins. I saw things a little more clearly. I had pushed the twins away, considering their birth was to blame for our family breakdown and for the loss of Cheniel. I never nursed and cared for them like a mother would but distanced myself from them, unable to show real love. It was a case of, 'if I couldn't have Cheniel, then I didn't want them'. I had four children and couldn't accept that I was capable of caring for one without the other. I never thought of Ian as part of that category, he was my first born and slightly older than the others so I suppose in a way I needed him as much as he needed me. It seemed the barrier that I used to protect myself as a small child was back in place, protecting me from the heartache and pain I was suffering. No doubt I had caused my children so much sorrow yet I felt so helpless; there was nothing I could do to change it.

At that stage of my life I was like a flower without water. I began to wilt and the world around me just seemed to get worse. After spending four happy years together, following a series of arguments, Eddie moved out and eventually returned to Colchester, as I always surmised that he would, and I began to go it alone. I had got to a stage where nothing mattered to me, the twins had become more difficult and I cared far less than I had ever done. A single night out lead to another and then another, until I was drinking so heavily I didn't even bother to go home at night, until eventually I lost the heart to return at all, leaving Ian to hold the family together. I remember I was so proud of him for attending college and holding a part-time job down yet I couldn't bring myself to go back home to him. Every time I walked through my front door into the house, I saw only three children and a great sadness hung over me. I felt the heartache that each one of them suffered; it was that which I couldn't bare. I had fought so hard to bring Cheniel home, but it was like building a giant jigsaw with one vital piece missing. Without it the picture wasn't complete.

My reasoning for leaving my children alone wasn't rational. I know that now, but at that time nothing in my life seem to matter.

Being sure that I couldn't make their lives any worse than I had, I met and married Smithy - a man that I had hoped would make a perfect father for them. Always in the back of my mind was the thought of building the ideal situation so that I could once again apply to the courts to bring Cheniel home.

—∞—

CHAPTER 10

Digging Myself a Deeper Hole

At first I thought Smithy was just what we needed, he seemed reasonably quiet, reserved and far more intelligent than he gave himself credit for. He had been born into a much higher status than I was, so I laid all my cards down on him; only later did I find that there was a side to him that I just didn't understand.

Our wedding day was chaos and our time together always seemed to include the presence of my sister, Carol. It was months before I realised that my children played an insignificant part in our married life and yet I had noticed that he placed Carol on a pedestal; far above any of us. Then one morning I woke up and began to take stock of our relationship. I couldn't remember how I had met him and couldn't for the life of me understand why I was with him, only that once again I had drifted into a relationship I knew I was going to have trouble getting out of. The fear I had of him gradually built up from the day I met him and far exceeded any love I felt for him. It seemed that overnight he had turned insanely jealous and terribly possessive, which resulted in us having awful fights. The alcohol he consumed both day and night impaired his thoughts and he would instantly become angry at the thought of me not possessing certain qualities that he thought I should have had. It soon became clear to me that he was emotionally unbalanced and hated the thought of being involved with me. Although he frequently told me that he loved me, I didn't believe him as the strongest emotion that he ever showed to me was hate.

He spoke of many things that I didn't understand and recalled horrific scenes from books that he had read - so he said. His explicit description of homicide was terrifying and his constant bragging of the ability to commit the same almost made me vomit. There was definitely something terribly strange about him; something that I couldn't put my finger on. He thought nothing of brandishing lethal weapons in front of my face and found great pleasure in putting his hands around my neck in order to restrict my breathing, so that he could watch me writhe. There was really nothing nice about him, yet Carol worshipped the ground he walked on. I got to think that maybe it wasn't such a good idea to invite her to Old Bolingbroke all those years ago. Whatever made me think she couldn't manage without me, I don't know! She was as callous as he was; so what on earth had I been thinking?

She always seemed to turn up when I was most vulnerable, when I felt sad and lonely and everyone else had forsaken me. So I regarded her as my best friend, the sister I wanted to look up to, someone whom I admired for her strength. But who was she really? It had been so long since our childhood that I had forgotten what she was really like. I remember vaguely when she introduced me to Smithy, it was like meeting an old friend, someone who had known me for years and knew me quiet well. It seemed like there was nothing I could tell him that he didn't already know. Although there was very little communication between us, anything we did say seemed to pass through Carol first and he seemed to know everything she had done and people that she knew.

I was lured into bed soon after meeting him. I'm not quite sure by whom, but I remember lying on his bed speechless, drunk and worse for wear, wondering what the hell I was doing there. Then suddenly out of the blue he proposed to me. I got the strangest feeling that I couldn't refuse, not because I loved him but because I felt such an overwhelming sense of trepidation. Although very few words were spoken, I felt threatened by him, even though he was acting the loving admirer.

I had spent all day in the Cherry Tree public house drinking lager until I couldn't drink anymore, so it's difficult for me to recall everything that happened that day.

I remember looking around his bedroom. It was cold and dark with a terrible smell of dog and damp in the air and resembled an old garage-type building that I could recall seeing when I was a small child; something that I would have mistaken for a boy's den, had I not known better. I wasn't sure at first if it was his bedroom, or just an old wreck of a building where he generally took loose women. I wondered at that point if he had already categorised me and expected more than I was willing to give. I felt ashamed for being there and wanted to leave straight away, but the strength of that inner fear felt so intense it seemed to paralyse me to the bone, so I knew I wasn't going anywhere. The fact that he had asked me to marry him hadn't quite registered but then my natural instinct kicked in and told me to think very carefully before I answered. We had nothing at all in common and

I was absolutely certain that I would live to regret it, but for the first time in my life I did the opposite to what I was renowned for - I allowed my head to rule my heart and made a decision I still feel saved my life. Before I accepted his sudden proposal of marriage, I took a long hard look at him. Although his eyes seemed fixed on my face, he looked vacant and the very second I opened my mouth to speak he bit furiously at my words until I gave him the answer he expected. Then he fell asleep instantly. Even at that moment I didn't feel safe to leave and my heart sank as I realised I had sentenced myself to a life of persecution. He wasn't the sort of character to let me walk out of that room without fulfilling my obligations, I sensed that well before I had realised that he had taken me home for one purpose... for keeps. We never resumed a normal relationship, he demanded sex and I performed without question. It was something I did automatically, switching off, feeling cold and empty; it felt the most natural thing in the world. I no longer felt embarrassed or uncomfortable and I felt no shame. In fact, I felt nothing; absolutely nothing.

I had never managed my life very well. Everything I touched seemed to fall apart and the life I had always wanted for my children never materialised, and I just kept on digging myself a deeper hole. I felt terribly guilty about leaving the children overnight in Old Bolingbroke and it was a while before I had sobered up and finally plucked up the courage to ask Smithy's permission to move them into the bungalow with us. Ian was adamant that he wouldn't leave, he loved it there and although we had struggled while we were there it was his home so he remained attending college and working part-time to help make ends meet. Occasionally I called in to see him.

It was at that stage of my life that I realised that I had failed him and no matter which way I turned I could not see a way to make amends.

For years I had tried to be a good mother but everything I did seemed to backfire, so I just stopped trying, telling myself that it was okay because I had tried so hard, yet failed. In my heart of hearts I just knew that I was doing wrong by them but I just couldn't find the strength to pull myself together. Regrettably I left Ian alone at Old Bolingbroke but took the twins with me to stay with Smithy and his mother in their bungalow at Ingoldmells, close to the sea on the east coast. The minute we arrived it was made perfectly clear that his mother was the head of the household and at times I found it difficult to understand where I fitted in; I had no household duties to perform and the twins became her responsibility. At times I felt like I was living with an old married couple, regularly invited to stay but deliberately made to feel uneasy.

His mother was as strange as he was and just as difficult to understand. It seemed that they had both led a very secluded life, yet something told me that there was so much more to their lives than they were willing to tell. The story of her wealthy father dying and leaving them destitute was repeatedly told, then celebrated with the fact that she had taken her father's recently bereaved widow to court and gained enough of his estate to obtain medical treatment for her terminally ill sister and enabled her to downgrade to the bungalow - something she once would have sneered at but had learned to appreciate. I wasn't surprised to learn that her father had always supplied them with a beautiful manor-type residence while he was alive but then he let them down when he died without making a will; his beautiful French wife inherited everything that they owned. A sympathetic Judge allowed them to keep enough funds to treat the cancer-riddled sister before she died and gave them a roof above their heads, but then he stripped them of everything they had gotten accustomed to. They were so familiar with the luxury that her father had afforded them that they thought of their loss as a total tragedy, so found it difficult to cope amongst people like me.

While living as his wife, I sensed a lot of fear inside Smithy - fear that his mother had put there. It seemed that ever since he was a small boy she had been drilling the same old stories into his head until they had become fixtures of his imagination and terrified him beyond belief. The very thought of dying from a heart attack like his father ruled his life and counting the years that he had left on this earth caused him to suffer greatly from anxiety. His mind had been filled with so many disturbing thoughts that he had recurring dreams that were so vivid they affected him for days. As an outsider I saw that his mother's suppression of certain memories caused her great problems, but not allowing Smithy to recall memories of his father and their life together caused greater problems for him. They both rejected any offer of help and the very thought of seeking treatment from a psychiatrist was regarded as totally unacceptable. His mother had previously made it clear to me that she felt ashamed that he had once been committed to a psychiatric ward, so ignored any familiar signs and watched him battle with the irritating symptoms of mental illness.

I was blinded by a make-believe situation and drifted from one day to the next, not realising how serious things were. We had only been married for a few months when our strange relationship went totally haywire. Following bouts of sexual aggressiveness, he became even more forceful and treated me with so much disrespect I could hardly bare him to touch me. Then the day came when he lost control altogether and, with his hands firmly wrapped around my neck, he raved like a lunatic and caused me to panic as the thought of dying flashed before me. I couldn't draw breath and as the room began to spin, I realised just how close I was to the point of no return. Everything I focused upon was totally distorted and the anger I felt within him terrified me; despite feeling nothing for him, tears rolled down my cheeks as I began to cry. As he pressed his thumbs hard against my throat, I prepared myself for death but something told me not to let go, I knew I was worth more than that so I did all I could to hang on, praying that at some point he would release me and I would breathe again. At times even his own mother vowed to get away from him but, like me, she was trapped by the same terrifying fear that kept us all there. No doubt he was unlike other men. Although he had been highly educated, he still remained the most unpredictable person I had ever met. I couldn't believe that someone who looked so kind and gentle could have been so cruel, yet the fear he created inside me was so strong that I could never remember feeling anything remotely similar. There was something about him that made him much more frightening to me than even my brother, John, or any other man that I had ever been in contact with. I sensed the strongest fear of death when I was around him and even at that stage of our relationship I knew that I was to experience far more suffering before our relationship reached the final peak of destruction. For hours I sat and cried, knowing that once again I had put myself into a situation that I couldn't get out of and desperately feared for my children's lives, as well as my own. I knew I had to leave him but there was something inside my head which told me to prepare myself before going headlong into a situation that I wasn't sure of. The short time that I had been married to him felt like years and in that time I had become aware of so many terrible things that he was capable of, yet I still couldn't find the courage to walk away from him. In time he began to act out all his sexual fantasies, becoming unmercifully cruel and far more perverted than he had originally been. Instead of trying to communicate with me normally, he would shout out sexual commands and, if I didn't respond, he fired up into a terrible rage and shook from head to foot with temper. With his fists clenched, he lashed out at me, unconcerned how much pain he caused me. I spent most of my time lying in his bed, where he had ordered me to remain until he had finished with me.

When I looked back to the kind of life I had lived before I had met him, I realised that in comparison it had not been so bad and I yearned to go back in time and yet I knew that once I had made the decision to leave him my life would never be the same again. Even so I never dreamt that when I did he would make it as devastating as he did. But, of course, I realise now that if I hadn't made that choice, I may not have lived to have told this story.

It was December 1995 and for obvious reasons Christmas just didn't feel the same; there was no excitement leading up to it and no merriment or Christmas cheer. The giving of gifts didn't seem important and our traditional Christmas lunch was replaced with a cold meat and pickle supper. I sought Smithy's permission to put up the Christmas tree and the few decorations that we had bought from Old Bolingbroke, but I had never seen them look so drab. That year he and his mother gave Christmas a whole new meaning. Although I was allowed to shop for toys for my children, I had never been made more conscious of it. I wasn't able to afford Skegness prices and, because he was such an attention-seeking person, he couldn't bare to allow me the time to shop around for cheap little stocking fillers, so I wasn't able to give my children much that year. All I wanted to do was to make my children happy but even the thought of that created so much violence within him. I was too frightened to stand up to him, so failed my children once again. It was at that point I decided to leave him. The question was; when?

Coming and going was nothing new to me, it was something I had done all my life. Only that time was different. I had already been made aware of the dangers that I faced, yet up to that moment I had never experienced telling a psychotic partner that I didn't love him so I was terribly uncertain of the way he would react and how things would turn out, so I trembled at the thought of telling him. For weeks I thought long and hard about nothing else and my mind kept on drifting back to when I considered my life to be so much simpler. As the New Year approached, I suddenly remembered my mother's words and gave lots of thought to the advice that she had always given me, 'Start the New Year as you mean to go on.' It was something I had always remembered her saying and for the first time in my life, those words actually made sense. I was scared and

I wondered if I had actually got the courage to take that initial step, I remember thinking to myself, 'I have brothers and the police station isn't too far away.' And, of course, there was the Magistrates Courts if I needed to apply for a protection order to keep him from harming us. But then I wondered, 'would that be enough to protect us from a man like him?' Nobody seemed to know him like I did, so I wondered if it would be possible to convince anyone that this quietly spoken, educated gentleman was capable of killing me. I didn't think so! There was a large part of me that wanted to believe that the law was on my side but the thought of failing to convince them that we needed protection, kept me his prisoner far longer than I would have been had I been confident that they were there for me.

Smithy's interpretation of my quiet nature was that I was cold and unfeeling and he informed anyone who came near me that I was bitter and frustrated - a remark I simply couldn't handle, so I spent a lot of my time crying over it. I felt ashamed when he told his friends that he thought more of Carol than he did of me and I started to really despise him when he openly announced that he should never have married me. What he didn't know was how much I wished he hadn't. Although it was very rare that I openly disagreed with Carol, we seemed to get along much better when Smithy wasn't around. Even though she didn't live with us, I remember her visiting me when he was at work and we would enjoy scornfully mocking him and relieved ourselves of the terrible animosity that he had caused between us. No matter how many hours we spent together, it always came down to the same thing - fear of his return and how I would safely get away from him.

Nothing seemed clear to me, everything around me felt unnatural, like I was living in a topsy-turvy world that I couldn't make sense of. For some unexplained reason Carol always tried to convince me that she was resilient to his threats and that she wasn't the least bit afraid of him; I could never understand that. At other times she gave me the impression that she was in league with him and laying some kind of trap for me, purposely to harm me. We had never got on one hundred per cent, despite what some people thought, and she had never treated me as an equal so I knew she'd be capable of damaging me any way she thought fit. She knew as well as I did how peculiar he was and yet, for some reason, she never paid a lot of importance to it so I always got the impression that she was exempt from any harm he may cause. This worried me more than anything, as she knew me better than most so had the power to destroy me if she had the will.

The more I thought about things, the more I worried about it and I suppose the stories that he had told me just added to those worries until the day came when I realised that the life they had built for themselves made mine and my children's so bad that I reverted back to the same nervous wreck that I had previously been. I couldn't clear my mind of the young teenage girl that he had boasted about abducting. He told me that she had special needs and was on the run; I wasn't sure I believed him yet I couldn't think of anyone more capable of doing such a thing. The full details of his acclaim constantly played on my mind, but as I pictured that thirteen-year-old girl, lost and frightened, I trembled at the thought of him having sex with her. I couldn't believe that he was telling me in such gory detail that he had taken a young girl off the streets purposely to have sex with her, knowing that she wouldn't understand it. For months I sat and wondered, even pondered about calling the police, but I suppose I was no different from thousands of others who regularly ignored tales like that. I constantly wondered about it and tried to understand why he would do such a thing: insanity, frustration or just sheer pleasure? I didn't know; what's more I didn't want to know. I suppose in a strange kind of way I felt sorry for him. I can't think of a single reason why I should have done but I know a very small part of me did. From that moment on I watched over my children like a cat watching a mouse, ensuring that he didn't go anywhere near them. I felt sorry for him but I didn't trust him. While I took my time in making that initial move; it was that which gave me the incentive to get away from him.

I had spent a lot of my time confined to his mother's bungalow so knew every nook and cranny. My instincts had warned me that more had happened there and I felt troubled with the uneasy cold, unearthly atmosphere that their home projected. I had felt uneasy at the best of times, but as I had got to know him my nervous disposition had gotten much worse so my tendency to remain indoors hidden away from their community seemed to come naturally. I felt extremely lonely and terribly unhappy. I became absent-minded and totally preoccupied with the thought of making life easier for him, but failed to consider my children or myself. The duty of being his wife seemed to include me in a masquerade of pretence that he and his mother had inhabited through the many years they had spent together, but it was something I found that I couldn't take part in. My future seemed a long way off and the thought of spending a whole lifetime with him almost drove me crazy, so for the first time since I had come to know him, I planned to break away from him. I knew that it wouldn't be easy and I absolutely dreaded the thought of him finding out before I had managed to get away, but I knew I had to do it; it was just a matter of how and when! I spent a tremendous amount of time trying to figure out how to get out of the situation without feeling the need to tell him. That was one of the most difficult things I had ever done. Making arrangements behind his back was nerve-racking and the thing was, I couldn't think of anyone I could turn to whom I could trust, so there was no-one I could approach for help. At that time everyone I associated myself with was either his social partner or, incredible as it seemed, an admirer of his. People knew so little about him and what they thought they knew couldn't have been further from the truth. Carol seemed to be the only person who knew many truths about him, but it was only when I informed her that I was leaving him that she chose to tell me that he had slashed his previous girlfriend's wrists when she tried to leave. It was just one more thing that she knew but failed to warn me about until it was too late. I was taking a risk, I knew that, but what I also knew was that if I stayed I would have been taking a much bigger risk. I didn't trust Carol, I never had, but once again she was the only one around when I was desperate and needed help. Despite the fact that she wasn't all together trustworthy, I knew under the circumstances I could count on her. She had always been pleased when my relationships had failed so I knew that she would welcome the chance to help me to see it through. She had never been shocked to hear me say, 'I'm leaving him'. I had said it so often I believed she expected it of me. She enjoyed the disturbance of my failed relationships and the aftermath that went with it, I think simply because it made her feel needed, and that time was no different from any other. Despite my better judgement, I still allowed her to take full control and, as usual, the whole thing backfired on me. It took months for me to pluck up the courage to call it a day. The hardest thing was to walk away from him knowing that it was one more relationship I had failed in. I knew that I had tried my utmost to make it work but when I finally accepted defeat, I cried like a baby. It was impossible trying to live a normal life with someone who had the characteristics of a psychopath. I never knew what to say or how to respond during his violent outbursts and when his personality changed, I became increasingly worried about our safety. He would suffer long bouts of silence, and then suddenly rear up into a monstrous and cruel ogre; he was absolutely terrifying. Carol had never seen him in a rage like that and even when I told her about him, she didn't respond the way I thought she would. At times she gave me the impression that she didn't believe me. Although she had never been any good at showing sympathy, I thought she might at least show a little concern but I was wrong. I really couldn't understand her, so much had happened in the short time I had known him yet she still treated him with the utmost respect and addressed him as 'Smithy darling'. I suppose in her defence it was difficult to believe that such a sociable, well-liked individual such as he could have been one of the most unpredictable, monstrous, psychopathic types who regularly attacked women like me. Admittedly, it was only after suffering at his hands that I realised that the most unlikely people could commit such gruesome attacks on unsuspecting individuals such as me. It was only at that time that I fully understood that there wasn't any particular type who was more capable than another of committing such crimes. They didn't have to be hard and callous like my eldest brother, John, to commit gross indecency and rape, and they didn't have to be unlike Smithy to commit gruesome attacks on the innocent. I remember feeling very disappointed in myself when I realised that, even after all my years of suffering, I still failed to recognise the individual most likely to cause me harm and I hated that weakness in me. I thought to myself many times, 'surely I should be able to see things more clearly' but it seemed I was so sure it would never happen to me again. I was blinded by certainty.

A few days before I left him, I did what I considered to be the most sensible thing and sought legal advice from a local solicitor. I told them parts of the story and because they were renowned for dealing with that kind of thing, it seemed like no big deal. They were particularly busy, rushed off their feet, and I noticed when it got to my turn that the office was about to close. I had been the last client in and, as I was leaving their very impressive office block, I got the distinct feeling that my visit had been an utter waste of time. I had found it really difficult to speak openly to a complete stranger and I felt that some things that I really needed to talk about were so personal I found it impossible to divulge everything. I left feeling very upset and embarrassed at the thought of being blamed for rushing headlong into a relationship, without first analysing who it was that I intended to marry. Ordering the twins to follow me, I walked away quickly, feeling belittled and utterly bewildered, clutching a bundle of formal notes I had acquired. I wondered what the hell I was doing there. It seemed that all I had achieved that day was to register myself as a statistic. I couldn't remember a single word that the solicitor had said and all that seemed important was the papers I held in my hand. I left the office block via the front entrance, which led me onto the main road where my car was parked. Having unlocked the car door, I knelt onto the driver's seat and leaned far enough over it to reach the back door catch and prised it open, allowing the twins to fumble their way onto the back seat. Then, without thinking, I drove straight to my home in Old Bolingbroke. It was only a couple of miles from the solicitor's office and yet the drive seemed to take forever and I cried all the way home, knowing that it was going to take a lot of toil and trouble to get through it. I wasn't sure what upset me the most, watching the twins' security disappear through my rear view mirror or knowing that I didn't have a clue what to do next. I thought I would feel a whole lot better after speaking to someone about him, but it seemed that involving one more person made me feel worse. I had been rushed in and out of an office to speak to a solicitor who didn't seem to have time for me and, in my opinion, didn't really care. Although I was allowed to speak out as much as I wanted in the short space of time that I was given, in comparison to all that had happened I had told them nothing. I remember that I felt so sad and lonely I didn't want to live through another day; life had become so difficult it felt like there was no other person in the world but me. I was afraid to go back to the bungalow and just wished that somehow the world could swallow me up. I thought about ways that I could get away, but even the thought of taking my own life was too much for me; I was a coward through and through. Running away was one thing but severing my strings to life was another. I knew I hadn't got what it took to do that. When I arrived back at Old Bolingbroke, I bathed the twins and tucked them up into their beds and made them a sandwich from the ingredients that Ian had left in the fridge and within no time at all they were fast asleep. I had expected Smithy to come looking for me as it was unusual for me to be out so late with the twins but, apart from Ian returning home from college, I saw no-one that night.

I was sat in the dark when Ian arrived home. He was surprised to see me but the smile on his face told me how pleased he was that I was there. I hadn't seen him for a while and, because Smithy was unpleasantly possessive, I had been too frightened to visit him. He sat down beside me knowing it was pointless asking me about Smithy - a nickname Ian had chosen for him when he first met him. Ian never liked him, even when he had tried to be nice to him. Ian understood more than I gave him credit for and, because I had raised him on a one-to-one basis for the biggest part of the seventeen years he had been on this earth, he knew me better than most and knew before I did that Smithy wasn't the right man for me. When I realised Smithy wasn't coming to look for me, I decided to stay on at Old Bolingbroke just for a few more days; I was at peace there. For the first time in my life I realised just how much life meant to me and how important it was for the children to be where they were happiest.

I tried to remember everything that the solicitor had said to me, though I recalled very little until I opened the letter I received in the post a couple of days later.

It quoted everything that I had told them and what they had advised and then it came straight to the point - the summons which they had already served on him. I felt instantly terrified, but the paragraph which frightened me the most was where it clearly stated where and when I had to attend court! I hadn't realised that I would have to attend as well. I had hoped it would all be dealt with in my absence, but I must have been crazy for assuming that. It was at that moment that I panicked, wishing that I hadn't taken any action against him at all. Lots of issues ran through my mind, but none which I could make any sense of. I thought about all the people I had come to know since I had moved into Lincolnshire and wondered why I still felt isolated. My whole life was in turmoil and I felt hopelessly detached from the rest of the world. I was alone and, for the first time in my life, I hated the very thought of it. My mind ran into confusion and I couldn't think. It was at times like that I couldn't see my way forward or allow myself to think back to the times when I was more fearful of him. For reasons I couldn't understand, my mind shut down and everything became a total blank. For a moment I stood still and tried to focus on everything that was around me, I felt myself trembling as my heart beat rapidly against the walls of my chest; for just a moment my whole world stood still. The sudden realisation that he could tap me on my shoulder at any moment scared the hell out of me and I broke into hysterics. For the first time in a long time I succeeded in working myself up into one of the most severe panic attacks that I had ever experienced. It was at that moment I accepted that my life with him was over. I couldn't go back, not then, not ever! After spending a few days away from him and his mother,

I began to feel a whole lot better in myself even though I knew I still had to finalise things. The court date was pending and the closer it got the more anxious I became. I guessed that he had already realised by then that I wasn't going back to the bungalow and I surmised that he didn't really care, but I was wrong.

On the day of the hearing I arrived in court early, about an hour before he did. Although I was accompanied by my solicitor, I was very nervous about seeing him and hadn't a clue what he would say to me, if anything at all. I wondered what he would think about me dragging his name through the courts and constantly told myself that he wouldn't dare make a scene in front of all the authoritative staff who was employed there. I was almost close to tears by the time he arrived, more so when I realised that he felt so confident that he hadn't even employed a solicitor to act on his behalf. He had this way of convincing people that he was cool, calm and collected and showed no reason for being anything different. Had I not known him better, even I would have been convinced that he had been summoned to court on false pretences. His show of innocence was obviously intended to deceive the magistrates and that's exactly what it did. I had only been inside the courtroom for five minutes when my application for a Protection Order was considered unnecessary. The accusations that I made carried no weight and were literally regarded as untrue. I sat inside the courtroom trying to take in everything that my solicitor was saying, recognising that the Magistrate who was deciding my and the children's fate was only interested in half of what was being said and placed no importance on the violence that had taken place between us. I wasn't surprised when it took a sudden afterthought to encourage the Magistrate to put a Restraining Order in place. But no matter what my solicitor said, the Magistrate wouldn't for the life of him attach a Power of Arrest to it, which basically told me that the order I was being granted wasn't worth the paper it was written on. I knew that and so did Smithy. The hearing was over within fifteen minutes, by which time I assumed that Smithy would accept that there was no going back. I wasn't sure that he would comply with the rules of the Restraining Order, but I was so desperate I wanted to believe that he would. I walked out of the courtroom really disappointed with the whole system. I was virtually in tears and felt angry at the fact that the authorities had believed him over me. I walked away with my head low, too ashamed to look up at anyone. Feeling really hurt and unprotected, I walked alongside my solicitor. He was well aware of the fear I had of Smithy and remained close by my side. He assured me that I would come to no harm if I allowed Smithy to leave the building before I did, as he could see that the hearing had not deterred him from harassing me. It was a good ten minutes before I had left the courtroom, as Smithy made it perfectly clear to me that he wasn't put off by the lame court order that had been put into place or my solicitor's presence and told me that he would be outside waiting for me! He behaved totally differently to how he had behaved in front of the Magistrate and was bursting with rage. By the time I had reached the foyer, his face was an awful crimson colour and displayed so much hate I feared for my life. Frightened to go any further, I stepped back, allowing my solicitor to move forward as he manoeuvred himself around in order to protect me. Smithy called out at the top of his voice, threatening to harm me and ordering me to his side. He repeatedly told onlookers that I was his wife, as if that gave him every right to make demands of me. But I had no intention of doing as he said; I had made a break from him so stood my ground firmly, knowing that he wouldn't give me up readily. I had hoped that my solicitor had enough power to command respect from him in order to persuade him to leave me alone, but his demand fell on deaf ears. My solicitor was definitely shocked by Smithy's threatening behaviour and couldn't believe the sudden change in him. The shock of witnessing a perfect example of a man with a split personality, exemplifying both good and evil, gave him the shakes and caused his voice to quiver as he urgently called out for assistance. I was devastated. After all the grief I had been put through in order to seek protection for myself and my children, everything seemed to have failed and I was back to where I had started. I couldn't believe it. I had just obtained a court order which wasn't worth the paper it was written on, so basically I had no protection at all and no way of acquiring any. I hurried out of the court yard, frightened and bewildered, hoping to get away from there before Smithy had the chance to follow me. I had seen him looking through my car windows earlier but, since he had been reprimanded for creating a scene, he had disappeared from view and I quickly left while I had the chance. I got into my car and looked around nervously. It took me a while to get my thoughts together and get the keys into the ignition. My hands were trembling so it took a second or two to start up the engine then I drove out of the court yard and headed towards town. I needed to purchase a few necessities from Skegness before going home, but what I hadn't expected was seeing Carol coming out of Lumley Road post office. She stopped and called me over, and I assumed in the time it had taken me to park the car and walk through the shopping centre that she may have seen Smithy already, as she seemed a little too intent on finding out what had happened in the courtroom. I didn't divulge too much, as I could never really be sure whose side she was on or what she really thought about me leaving him. Sometimes she gave me the impression that she understood and at other times she seemed to switch over to his way of thinking. I left out as much detail as I could and went automatically into shopping mode. After visiting a couple of supermarkets to purchase what bits of food I needed, she persuaded me to go freezer shopping with her. I didn't really want to go and gave the excuse that I had to rush back to collect the twins from Pat, my neighbour who had volunteered to babysit while I was attending court. But Carol was so persuasive I went along with her, knowing that once again she was just using me. She had previously created a pattern of behaviour in me where I would automatically respond to her every whim without ever questioning it. Unfortunately I was raised to believe that that was the way things were done and I hadn't at that time developed the initiative to change it.

When I finally managed to get away from her and I was driving home, I felt an overwhelming feeling of desperation. It seemed that no matter who I approached for help, there was no-one who was willing to put themselves out for me. I had approached all the right authorities who at one time would have proven themselves reliable, but at that time I had found them utterly disappointing. I kept on wondering what it was about me that these people didn't seem to like. Was it something that I had done or said that encouraged them to mistrust me, or did I look the type of person who intended to deceive? I wasn't sure. Sometimes I felt that it was simply because I was a young woman being judged by a man, although I preferred to think not. Now I realise the reason for their seemingly biased opinion of me was simply because they didn't understand me. I wasn't able to express myself as clearly as some, so when I faced an opponent like Smithy, I was unable to challenge them respectfully, and I was frowned upon for using inappropriate expressions. My mother always said 'actions speak louder than words', but unfortunately inside a courtroom they are inadmissible. There was no-one inside that courtroom who understood how the epilepsy and anxiety depression had affected me and nobody concerned themselves as to why I was so inconsistent when put under pressure. I understood that my emotional outbursts were inconsistent with my appearance, but what really hurt was the fact that I put all my trust in the Queen's Counsel, just to be snubbed by his ignorance. I understood only too well that there was a certain amount of stigma attached to any psychological illness, but I had been assured so many times that inside a courtroom this wasn't the case. Unfortunately I saw no proof of that.

When Smithy had been acquitted of any wrongdoing; I had this terrible feeling that I would receive far more grief from him than I had originally expected. He had nothing to fear, no order that really meant anything and no law to discourage his violence. I was sure I knew him well enough to know that he would seek revenge on me, not just for taking him to court for something he thought he was innocent of, but also for the fact that I had the audacity to leave him for it. I had no idea what was going to happen next, but for every impending thought that raced through my mind; I had thought of nothing as severe as the action he finally took.

—w—

CHAPTER 11

Hurt and Unprotected

I arrived back at Old Bolingbroke totally exhausted. Most of my energy had been drained by my incapacity to think rationally and I felt weak at the knees. I gazed across the greenbelt and allowed my body to relax as I drove steadily onto the soggy grass verge opposite to where I lived. It wasn't raining but there was evidence of it on the roads. It seemed that I had just missed a heavy downpour and, although everywhere was wet and muddy, it felt much more pleasant than the courtroom I had come from. I sat quietly enjoying the privacy of my own car, watching the last droplets of rain trickle down my windscreen while I made an attempt to buck up before I made a move to collect the twins from Pat's house. I sat listening to the finishing tones of UB40 singing their version of *Kingston Town*, before I turned off the radio and climbed out of my car. My legs felt sluggish and I really didn't feel like moving, but I knew that I couldn't sit there forever. The twins had spotted me crossing the road and were waving frantically through Pat's living room window. They were really excited when they greeted me at the front door. I could rarely afford sweets but on the odd occasions when I had to go out on business, I treated them to a small tube of Smarties. They had become accustomed to that and were pestering me for them. They were funny kids really; so difficult to take care of, but pleasant to come home too. As I walked through Pat's front door into her living room I could barely hear a word that she was saying, as the twins were eagerly chatting away tying to gain my attention. Feeling exhausted, I flopped down in the armchair closest to me as Pat thoughtfully handed me a hot cup of coffee and suddenly the twins fell silent as I pulled them up onto my knee. I sat back feeling very relieved that the day was almost over. Cupping the hot drink in my hands, I sipped at my well-earned coffee and let out a long, extended sigh of relief. The clock on the mantel displayed 4:15pm. Although this seemed typical of my life, I couldn't believe that it had taken a whole day to accomplish absolutely nothing. I sat silent for a while listening to Pat and Brian arguing over the television channels. It seemed that Brian had been at home all day and the only way he could escape boredom was to generate a row with Pat so that he had an excuse to leave the house. I left their house with the twins just at the right moment, but as soon as I had left I was closely followed by a very frustrated Brian. I knew he'd follow me, he always did. At times we got on like a house on fire but I could never understand why he preferred to sit in my house rather than his own. We had always confided in each other but at times when I preferred to be alone I would sense a deep sadness in him, so spent a lot of my time housing his sorrows. He was a good friend but sometimes I felt that he was a little imposing and I was too soft with him. He always left around midnight after consuming most of my cigarettes and a fair amount of brandy, by which time I was too drunk to worry about my own problems. With a full belly of brandy and a couple of whisky chasers, Smithy and all his threats were the furthest from my mind. What I didn't realise was just how conscious I should have been of them. By the time I had secured the doors and stoked up the fire in the hearth, it had turned 1am, but I liked to keep the fire burning to ensure that we had hot water for the morning. Having replaced both the spark and nursery fireguard, I wasted no time in going to bed. As soon as my head hit the pillow, I was asleep. Understandably by the following morning I suffered from the most violent headache. Feeling very sorry for myself, I poured out a hot cup of coffee from the percolator and lit a cigarette. When Carol phoned, I snapped and snarled at her. She seemed rather cheerful, considering, and took me by surprise when she asked if I wanted to go out that night. It was merely for the sake of peace that I accepted, but I didn't really know for certain that I would be going as it meant that I had to ask Ian to babysit and I didn't like doing that. When I finally put the phone down I looked around the house. It was deadly silent. Ian hadn't long left for college and I had just that minute put the twins onto the school bus, so I was able to sit and think about yesterday. I sat down on the beautiful, charcoal blue dralon suite that my brother, Andrew, had given to me when his marriage had broken down and I gazed through our large picture window at the greenbelt that stretched for miles. I took particular notice of the recently decorated walls that surrounded me and, for just a second, I remembered the terrible fall that broke my toes when I was struggling to complete the decor of that place single-handedly. I cringed as I suddenly realised that my toes hadn't quite healed and remember thinking that I must have been crazy to have taken on something as big as that hoping to get it all finished in a matter of weeks. That was the kind of person I was though - strong, independent and determined. That's why I couldn't understand why I had left such a beautiful place to live in that awful bungalow with Smithy. Sometimes I had wondered if I was genuinely capable of making rational decisions as very often I got things so terribly wrong, which often resulted in the people closest to me getting hurt.

A large part of my past flashed before me and I could have cried buckets, but somehow I held on to what seemed to be a mountain of pressure while every single memory slowly disappeared in a cloudy mass of cigarette smoke. Then I did just about anything to take my mind off things. When Ian came home he didn't seem to be put out when I asked him to babysit. Although I knew that I shouldn't have relied on him, something told me to go out that night and I felt drawn to the telephone. Carol was thrilled when I called her to tell her that I was almost ready, but still I remained anxious. She tried to convince me that I had nothing to worry about as Smithy hadn't been seen in the Cherry Tree for some time. It was his usual haunt, but it was mine and Carol's too. I felt really unsure that going out was the best choice, but I didn't want him to think that I was hiding away just because I was frightened of him. At the same time I didn't want to walk headlong into trouble either, so instead of going straight to the Cherry Tree, we met at the Dunes so I could put my feelers out, but when I arrived I could see that the place was empty. I met Carol in the bar and the minute that I saw her, we looked across at each other and howled with laughter. It was like walking into a morgue and made me feel worse than I was already feeling.

It seemed that the Cherry Tree had put a good act in place and had robbed the Dunes of its regulars so we did no more than have a quick drink and left. When we arrived at the Cherry Tree, it was overcrowded. It wasn't easy to find a parking space and as one car pulled out of the car park another pulled in, until eventually I was lucky enough to find an empty space. I parked two rows back, in front of the main entrance, switched off the ignition and climbed out of my car. I walked nervously through the main entrance into the ladies' room. This gave me time to calm my nerves and raise my guard so that I could prepare myself for any confrontation I may have to deal with. As I discreetly made my way through the crowded pub, I noticed that Smithy wasn't sitting in his usual place and strangely no-one quizzed me about our separation, which told me that they were already aware of it. I suppose in a way that made going in there a lot easier for me. I knew at some point some individual would take a pop at me and blame me for the whole thing, as they didn't know him as well as I did. I must admit I wasn't too worried about what the locals thought, as most of them were self-confessed alcoholics and didn't really care who was to blame.

When I approached the bar, I was immediately served by a rather mature gentleman whom I had never seen in there before. He nodded courteously to me which made a welcoming change from the usual standard of bar person, who normally served me with a drink then rushed over to the next person without even acknowledging me. I thought he was dressed particularly smartly for the Cherry Tree. As I began to pay a little more attention to him, I noticed that the clothing he wore was a rather exquisite design from the Bird Cage, an exclusive boutique in Skegness. He carried the clothes well and, as I admired his persona, I paid slight attention to the rather exuberant diamond ring that he wore on the middle finger of his right hand; P.S. - my husband's initials. Although I felt sure he couldn't have the same name, I spent quite a considerable amount of time just watching him, wondering if his sudden appearance was an omen for disaster. I hadn't the nerve to ask him what his name was so I reluctantly asked Carol to find out instead, but it was no surprise to find that she already knew him. I was almost struck dumb when she suddenly yelled out at the top of her voice, 'Oh, Pete!' Then she did it again. I felt so embarrassed I got really angry with her, but it was too late she had already blurted it out and added, 'My sister wants to know if you're married.' It was loud enough for the whole pub to hear and I became so embarrassed I just didn't know which way to turn. I hated the way she belittled me when she thought fit. I was really shocked when I heard him say, 'Yes, I am, but I'll get divorced if she will.' At first I thought he was just having a laugh, but when he approached me and asked me to marry him, I didn't know what to say. I knew in the eyes of the law I was married to Smithy, but I didn't feel married. I never had, so I just replied, 'I'm sure you wouldn't want to do that... would you?' Moving closer towards me, he whispered, 'If you will, then I will.' I could sense by his mannerisms that he meant every word that he said, but it wasn't that that I wanted. When he stood next to me, he made me feel quite amorous; I could almost taste the aroma of his exquisite aftershave and I was immediately lured into temptation. I wasn't looking for a partner and I had no intention of getting married again, but for reasons I couldn't understand

I felt drawn to him. Peter was fifteen years my senior, not as well spoken as I would have liked, but his mannerisms were kind-of okay. I got to thinking how bad my life had been with Smithy and how it had been for my children, then suddenly I found myself wondering if this man might be more capable of giving me and my children what I expected from life. But I was petrified. Up until that moment, I had experienced nothing but heartache. My whole life had been one continuous struggle and, although I knew without a strong and reliable figurehead I would never get it right, I knew that I couldn't afford to make any more mistakes. Desperate to know what the initial 'S' on his ring stood for, I found myself talking to him on and off for most of the evening. I was attracted to him but repeatedly told myself that if his surname as much as resembled Smithy's, I would avoid him like the plague. When I eventually plucked up enough courage to ask about the initial 'S', he quickly replied 'Senior', then rhythmically spelt out his name 'S-E-N-I-O-R.' The perfection of rhythm told me that he had recited it more than once and I began to wonder if he might have perfected it on countless women before reciting it to me. It was at that moment that I began to wonder if I was doing the right thing by just talking to him. He was very swift on his feet, dancing from one side of the bar to the other as he casually collected glasses from the tables as a favour to his best friend, Steve, the landlord of the Cherry Tree. There were never enough staff to man the bar and Steve found it difficult to keep up with his customers' heavy consumption of alcohol, so often contacted Peter to help him with the bar duties. Although I had never met Peter before, I put it down to being controlled. Even when Smithy had ordered me to accompany him to the Cherry Tree, he never allowed me to socialise or take part in any conversations that he got involved in, which resulted in me staying close by his side most of the time, taking no particular notice of anyone.

Time had never seemingly passed as quickly as it did that night. Before I knew it, the towels had been spread across the beer pumps and Steve was ringing the huge brass bell which was attached to the bar and calling 'Time!' I drank what was left of my drink and waited around for Carol to finish hers. She had the terrible habit of ordering two pints of lager to my half at the very last minute, so she was constantly asked to drink up. I was usually bored out of my head waiting around for her, but on that night it felt different. I was in no hurry to leave and, while Carol said her long drawn-out goodbyes to each member of the bar staff, I said goodnight to Peter and left the pub via the back door and returned to my car. I was devastated to find that while I had been inside the pub, my car had been trashed. Both the front and back lights had been smashed and there were fragments of glass all over the ground, the wiper blades had been bent and twisted out of shape and the rear tyres punctured. The lingerers instinctively gathered around. Most of them were highly intoxicated yet they still tried to give unrealistic explanations of how the damage had been caused, but I wasn't stupid. They liked Smithy; he was one of the crowd, so to speak, so they did their best to protect him. I knew that he was responsible for the damage and wasn't surprised at his destructive aggression. He had already made it obvious to me that he was disturbed, so I knew from that moment I wasn't going to be safe. I stood looking over my shoulder first one way then the other, feeling very uneasy, wondering if he was out there watching me.

I stood in the car park amongst a crowd of drunks who called themselves 'his friends' and I wondered what the hell I was doing. I had never felt so miserable. Although I knew he was solely responsible for his own actions, I couldn't stop thinking what a waste of time the existing court order was. I knew without the attachment of Power of Arrest he wouldn't adhere to it, but he was a little shrewder than the Magistrates and came out of that court room free to do what he liked. When the crowd eventually dispersed, I walked slowly over to Carol's car and noticed that her new Vauxhall Nova was totally unaffected. I remember wondering if she had known before she had asked me out what was going to happen. No doubt I felt paranoid; so much had happened during that past year, I was very wary and felt that I couldn't trust anyone. I didn't argue with Carol that night but I do remember purposely insinuating that she had previously been aware of his intentions. Strange as it seemed, she didn't react. That was unusual for her. Instead she offered to drive me home and of course I accepted. It seemed totally unfair and I felt really angry, not just with Smithy but with the Magistrate who had found it difficult to believe that Smithy was something of a psychopath. In my eyes the Magistrate was as much to blame as he was. I believed that he could have prevented it from happening, had he not judged Smithy solely by his appearance.

—〰—

CHAPTER 12

Too Tired to Care

By the time I had arrived home, it was way past midnight and I felt very uneasy. I did my usual checks around the house and looked in on my children who were fast asleep in their beds. It was at those particular moments that I felt really guilty. In the past I had devoted my whole life to them but when I became desperate for a little respite, I found it impossible to find sitters who were willing to risk looking after the twins. Each time I had approached the Social Services, they had treated me with so much contempt and couldn't stress enough how the twins were my own responsibility and regularly informed me that it was my duty as their mother to find an adequate caretaker for them if I needed respite. I regularly argued with them and tried to point out how difficult the twins were and how exhausted I had become, but they just kept on reminding me that they didn't like to categorise children who had behaviour issues. So I felt that it was partly due to that, that I couldn't obtain the correct support from anywhere. I constantly felt that they much preferred to criticise my ability to care for my children, rather than accept that my care was of an unusually high standard but that I was dealing with two children who were virtually uncontrollable. I could understand where the social workers were coming from as before I gave birth to the twins, I too frowned upon parents who seemingly couldn't cope with their own children. But after experiencing the differences between what I considered to be the excellent behaviour of my two older children, Ian and Cheniel, and the unaccountable behaviour of Kyle and Allishia, I showed much more compassion to the parents who tried hard to care for their children with similar behaviour patterns to the twins. I knew it wasn't ideal leaving Ian alone with the twins, but life proved so difficult that I managed the best way I knew how, hoping I would get through the day-to-day struggle of trying to raise boisterous twins when all the odds were against me. As usual I went to bed crying, feeling very sorry for myself... but more so for my children.

The following morning I got up late and rushed around the house like a lunatic desperately trying to dress the twins, give them their breakfast and get myself ready in time to leave the house as soon as the school bus arrived to take the twins to school. I felt absolutely worn out and noticed that I was snapping at them more than usual. I didn't want them to miss the bus, as I desperately needed to relieve myself of their presence while I tried to sort out the car. I didn't want to leave it outside the Cherry Tree any longer than necessary, so the minute the bus arrived I grabbed their coats from the cloakroom and rushed them out through the front door and down our garden path. I gave them a quick kiss and a gentle squeeze before guiding them up the steep steps of the school bus, and felt utter relief once the bus had pulled away from the stop. The twins waved frantically through the windows as I kissed the tips of my fingers and blew them each a handful of heartfelt kisses, before I spun around and ran as fast as I could back up the garden path. I made a beeline for the telephone and quickly phoned for a taxi. Not surprisingly, they were all out on school runs so I hung around the house for a while - about an hour to be precise - just enough time to smoke a cigarette and make myself a coffee. When the taxi arrived I ran out of the house and slammed the back door shut. I never did lock it; things had always been safe in Old Bolingbroke so I had never felt that there was ever a need.

I travelled to Ingoldmells to take another look at my car and go in search of a mechanic who was willing to tow my car back to his garage and repair it for me, all at a price I could afford and on that same day. At first it seemed an impossible task, as none of the local garages wanted to put themselves out, but eventually I came across a small, back street garage and a mechanic who obviously needed the work. He was more than willing to repair it and try to do it in the time specified. I was taking a chance but I left the car keys with him and just hoped that when I returned it would be fixed and ready to go. I was shocked when I saw it on the road ready and waiting; I could have cried. It wasn't much of a car, just an old banger so to speak, but at that time it was our lifeline and we couldn't have managed without it. As soon as I got behind the wheel I drove straight to Friskney to visit Carol. I wanted her to know that it had been repaired so that she could inform Smithy, and of course to see her face when I pulled up in it. But before she had realised how I had gotten there, she had opened her front door to me and said, 'I've been thinking, you might as well write the car off as pay out to have it repaired.' She wallowed in the thought of me and the kids being stranded. Old Bolingbroke was miles away from anywhere, and those who lived there desperately needed their own transport otherwise it meant that they had to rely on other people, in which case I would have had to rely on her. She had always enjoyed that as it gave her power over me. She had always been able to manipulate me into doing things that I hadn't really wanted to do, but since I had bought my own car I had become much more independent and spent far less time with her than she would have liked. When she first opened her door and saw me standing there, she didn't say a lot about Smithy or what she thought about the damage that he had caused, but there again she didn't have to. Her acrimonious manner said enough. I can't remember there being many times when I was glad to be who I was, but at times like that I really appreciated the fact that I had been bred into a far better person than she had, as I was able to walk straight by her, giving her nothing more than a self-satisfied grin as I walked into the kitchen and made myself a cup of coffee. She didn't say anything more and I didn't expect her to, but something told me that things were never going to be the same between her and me. I knew only too well that I shouldn't have trusted her but she was my sister and, like always, I turned a blind eye to everything that had happened and went about my life as I had always done. After all, I figured that if that was the worst that was going to happen to us, then we would definitely be okay. But I had been wrong so many times before and it was only a few weeks later that I found I was wrong again. I returned home wondering why I felt the way I did about her, then I realised I had made a huge mistake socialising with her yet I was lonely and there was no-one else who I could relate to. Apart from living my life from day to day, doing what was socially expected of me; my life was monotonously dull and didn't seem to have any meaning. I don't remember how many times I had wished I was more like her, carefree and generally outspoken, but that was one of those days when I took a good look at myself and thanked God I was nothing like her. It was one of those very few moments I was glad to be myself. Despite her picking fault and throwing insults at me, I was glad to be me. In Carol's estimation she was 'Miss Perfect' and I was her underdog; a typical reject. She had a quirky kind of way of making me feel inferior and caused me to be unpopular with so many people, yet I still couldn't find the courage to battle with her. I always knew that I could be nothing like her and yet there had still been times when I was so envious of her inner confidence that I regularly wondered what it would be like just to be her for a day.

The next time I spoke to Peter Senior he was selling perfumes and cosmetics from a heavily congested market stall. I had arranged to meet Carol at 'The Fantasy Island Pleasure Park' at Ingoldmells and had decided to walk around with her, knowing that he worked there. It was a beautiful sunny day and the crowds thickened as morning stretched into the afternoon. I was unusually hot and not in the best of moods. I suffered from a terrible headache and put it down to a side effect of the epileptic seizure which I had suffered the night before. The twins had been playing me up and their school bus had arrived late. Combining everything, it had started out as one hell of a day, yet the minute I saw him my mood changed as I felt the thrill of excitement. Carol was her usual self and tried to steal the limelight with her obtrusive manner but for once she didn't worry me and I felt quite confident that this was one I didn't have to compete for. As we manoeuvred around the indoor market store, she immediately delved into his clothing stock, ransacking rail upon rail of fashion wear. She was embarrassing most of the time but I felt that she deliberately emphasized her ignorance, knowing that I would feel humiliated by it. I immediately suggested that we should leave and made the excuse that I didn't feel too well, but as usual she ignored me and gave out one of her penetrating squeals of delight as she recklessly searched through rail upon rail of beautiful garments. I cringed with embarrassment as she pulled individual items from the protective polythene that covered them and held them against her, proclaiming that they would fit her. Unaware of her selfish intentions, Peter suggested that she might try them for size and directed her to a small changing area at the back of the stall. I became more and more enraged at her behaviour and continually apologised for her sudden invasion of his ware. I showed my embarrassment by shying away from him and his stall, only to find that he followed me closely, totally ignoring the fact that Carol was there at all. Suddenly she emerged from the back of the stall and suggested that she might keep the large pile of clothing that she held in her arms, and to my surprise he agreed without question. I was mortified and felt my anger rise from the pit of my stomach to my throat. I repeatedly apologised for her ways and tried to cover my embarrassment by telling him that I hated the way she used certain situations and people to gain what she could. It was something that she had always done but, despite being told, she never changed her ways. She nursed the large pile of jumpers and blouses in her arms, failing to understand that she was robbing him of his livelihood. Then I wondered, even if she had been thoughtful enough to understand that, would she have offered to pay for them? I don't think so. I don't know what attracted me to Peter Senior, whether it was because we were the two opposites or simply because I believed in the tarot card readings and horoscopes that Carol regularly hurled at me. From somewhere sprung the initials P.S. and it seemed that I spent most of my time trying to piece together something that wasn't really there. At first I didn't believe a word of it, but then she caught me at an all-time low and convinced me that the tall, dark stranger with the initials P.S. whom she regularly spoke about was Smithy, so I was naive enough to marry him and when that didn't work. I was totally convinced that it was Peter Senior. I really don't know what was going on inside my head. But it certainly wasn't normality, I am certain of that now.

Peter Senior was a strange type of fellow who regularly insulted people without offending them and called out repetitively to passers-by in a bid to sell his wares. But one thing I really liked about him was that he showed empathy to the vulnerable. He had a sympathetic ear and so much regard for people with Down's syndrome. That, above everything, helped him to gain my full admiration. I began seeing him regularly soon after that; at first it was just a few hours a day and then it extended itself to a few days a week. We seemed happy and relaxed in each other's company and found that our need to see each other became so overpowering that we spent hours talking to each other over the telephone in between dates. He finally moved in with me and the children at Old Bolingbroke a couple of months later, when I gave him the ultimatum, 'Leave your wife or forget it.' I explained to him that I wasn't willing to play second fiddle to anybody. I had done it before but I wasn't willing to do it again, so I gave him just under a week to decide. I had hardened by that time and thought; if I was to start the relationship as I intended to go on, then it might work. I made a conscious effort to change from the submissive type of woman that I was to the more domineering type, hoping that somewhere in between I would reach a happy medium. Our sex life never reached an all-time great, but neither of us placed any importance on it. Having spoken openly of our past experiences, we kind of shied away from the sexual side of our lives and never really explored each other as we should have. I made it known to him from the beginning of our relationship that I wouldn't tolerate being forced into any type of sexual activity or made to feel obliged, so I guess that was the reason why he never approached me and why we never became naturally impulsive lovers. I always thought that I loved him, but the truth was I still didn't know what true love was. I had overwhelming feelings for my children and would have died for them, but as far as men were concerned I think I was incapable of loving them.

Peter Senior and I lived at Old Bolingbroke happy in the thought that we would be together forever and gradually moved on with our lives. We turned our back on Ingoldmells and all the sad times that we had experienced, and I concentrated on the happiness of my children. Within no time at all I had noticed that their smiles had returned to their faces and that they had begun to relax more. Once again we all learned how to have fun and spent hours playing games like we used to. It seemed that our lives had returned to normal and we were happy again. Peter continued trading. He had had to abandon his market stall to be with us and had lost most of his stock to his wife, but he remained positive and never once looked back. After three months I felt that we were really going somewhere, but then something strange happened and I couldn't get my head around it. Out of the blue I received the most bizarre telephone call from Carol. She had been out socialising and telephoned me on the pretence that she was worried about me. I was surprised by her sudden concern and questioned her reason for calling, as her tone of voice did not seem to fit with the connected events that she informed me of. She seemed hesitant but nevertheless I listened patiently as she informed me about her encounter with Smithy, which had apparently taken place only a few minutes before she had telephoned me. It wasn't her normal line of conversation and her voice began to waver a little, so naturally I thought that she was intoxicated and only concentrated on parts of the conversation. I ignored a lot of what was said as she spoke incoherently and I found it so difficult to understand her, until she placed so much emphasis on her next sentence and blurted out, 'He's gonna fukin' kill ya!' Shocked at what she had said, I immediately fell silent and listened to her breathing heavily down the phone while she struggled to deliver her next sentence: 'Lock ya winders and bolt ya dooers.' There was a terrible silence while I thought about what she had said, wondering when she was going to announce that it was all a joke, but she never did. Instead I felt a sudden rush of adrenaline as she dominantly said, 'I'm not jokin'. He fuckin' means it, Marie, he's gunner fuckin' kill ya.' Her voice sounded very strange, different to how I had always known it, but I still couldn't be sure that she was being serious. She had told me so many lies in the past that it was difficult for me to believe her, even when it was most crucial. But then as usual she got angry and hurled so much abuse at me that I couldn't take it all in. 'A fuckin' shattered glass, the fuckin' Cherry Tree, Smithy and the fuckin' kids' was all that had registered with me. Each statement that she made sounded more intimidating than the other, as if she was enjoying it. Then there was a sudden calmness about her as if I had nothing much to worry about and automatically she returned to what I would have perceived to have been her normal line of conversation, and asked, 'You guin' out tomorrow?' I was baffled and wondered what on earth she was trying to do to me. I slammed the phone down and burst into tears, not just because of the fear I had of Smithy but also because of Carol's sick sense of humour. Her ability to lie about such things was incredible. Although she seemed to find it amusing that she had left me in such a state, I felt petrified. Peter Senior tried his utmost to comfort me but I knew that I'd need more than a shoulder to cry on to get around that one.

Although I took precautions in locking the doors and securing the windows that night, I carelessly relaxed during the days that followed and allowed my children to go to the park with their friends while I pottered around the house like I always had. Occasionally my mind drifted back to some of the things that she had said, but foolishly I placed no importance on them. I constantly told myself that if her warning had been genuine then she would have informed the police well before phoning me; I felt sure of that. But after spending many days and nights trying to reason with myself, I became doubtful and constantly told myself that she had no cause to worry me unnecessarily. So why would she say those things? I tried my utmost to understand her but she was the most complex of creatures and always seemed to baffle me. Although it was difficult to get to the bottom of her at the best of times, it suddenly occurred to me that she may not have been warning me, but in a roundabout way may have been threatening me. Maybe that was the reason why her voice didn't seem to coincide with what she had said... I just couldn't understand what was going on. I had wondered many times if she had gotten herself involved with Smithy, but I had been too trusting to doubt her. Even at that late stage I allowed my emotions to cloud my thoughts and never once doubted her loyalty, but then like a flash of light I began to realise that she was my worst enemy! For her to be free of him, she needed me to go back to him. I was the bait which she used to keep herself free from his clutches. Initially she had used me to entice and attract him, solely to keep his attentions away from her. She had been happy to play the field when he had been one of her suitors, but when she became bored she helped to trap me for the admirer she no longer had use for, knowing that he was dangerous. I believed that the time had come when he saw right through her and gave her a choice. Her decision was to help instigate a crime that may not have happened had it not been for her.

It had been an exceptionally hot summer's day and my body was overheating from all the hours I had basked in the sun. The twins had just returned from school and had raced each other up the garden path, laughing and giggling their way towards the front door, followed by their dear little friend, Adele, who I took care of on Wednesdays and Fridays. Her father was employed as a special needs teacher and her mother was a nursery nurse at the Butlins Holiday Camp in Skegness. Being relatively new to the village, they had been unable to find a permanent sitter for Adele, so I volunteered and found myself caring for her even when the children weren't at school. As I greeted them I watched all three run through the house and listened to the heavy sound of footsteps as they ran up the stairs to get changed. I realised that was my cue to get up and make my way to the kitchen. I felt a little light-headed as I carelessly removed myself from the sun lounger and slowly walked towards the back door, and realised that I had spent far too much time in the sun that day. I entered the kitchen by the back door and felt instantly relieved by the coolness of the room, and helped myself to a cold drink from the fridge. As usual the twins were arguing and I could hear the competitiveness in their voices, but I knew only too well that it didn't pay to get involved unless it was absolutely necessary. I had learned the hard way and found that 'least said soonest mended'. It was unusual for me not to have dinner ready for them when they came home from school, but for no apparent reason on that day I hadn't. It took me all of twenty minutes to deep fry some fish fingers and prepare a side salad, by which time they had finished arguing and were sitting at the table eating. The concoction of tomato ketchup and salad cream dressing made their day and it seemed by the time they had left the table they were wearing more than they had eaten, but at least they had refrained from arguing. Within minutes of eating their dinner, they had carelessly tipped their dirty plates into the kitchen sink and made a beeline for the back door. From the outhouse I heard them call out in unison, 'Can we go to the park, Mummy?' I grabbed a tea towel and ran to the back door, by which time they had reached the bottom of the garden path and were running as fast as they could towards the old Bolingbroke Castle ruins. I called out at the top of my voice, 'Be good and don't leave the park! I'll pick you up at six. Are you listening, Kyle?' He looked back at me over his shoulder, so I knew that he had heard me, and I waved just like I always did. Although the twins where sometimes difficult they knew their boundaries - what I allowed and what I didn't - so were gone before I knew it. It was an endearing sight watching them chase along the hedgerows of Old Bolingbroke. It seemed like the only place left in the world where children roamed free in their wellington boots during the height of summer and amused themselves with simple blades of grass. Even when they were out of sight, I could hear the trail of laughter as they desperately tried to perfect the warbling sound I myself learned as a child. I smiled happily to myself as I walked down the garden path to close the gate. Catching the distant sound of their voices, I listened with intense wonder and thought how lucky I was to experience motherhood. I had been blessed and, although I had often found life difficult, I was grateful for the gift of children. I glanced across at Peter who was still basking in the sun and hadn't changed position since I had last looked at him. Although the day was cooling down, it was still warm and I could see the sun's rays shining towards the back end of our garden. In another half an hour he would be lying in the shade complaining that he was cold. I found it rather amusing that he complained so much about so little, so I did my utmost to cheer him up by squirting him with a washing up bottle filled with warm water. He wasn't generally the type to play around but since he had met me he had done a lot of things that he had never done before, so took a good soaking all in good part. He chased me around the garden and I got wet too, but I found it hilarious; it had been a long time since I had felt so relaxed and I laughed so much that I almost cried.

—∿—

CHAPTER 13

Kidnapped and Prepared to Die

I find it difficult to remember everything that happened that day, but I do recall Ian being at work and remember that I hadn't seen him since he had left for college early that same morning. Yet, strangely enough, I still remember the sudden screech of car wheels that attracted me to the front window. As I stood for a while, I watched not one but two strangers pull their cars to a halt at the side of the road, opposite our house. It wouldn't have seemed so unusual had they been known to me, but because they weren't I worried aimlessly. Both drivers seemed to be in a desperate hurry and, although they drove separate vehicles, they left together in only one, leaving the other car abandoned at the side of the road. Although I didn't recognise the men, I noticed that their demeanour was somewhat unusual for that area but still I didn't seem to grasp what was happening and tried to clear my mind of the event. Occasionally through the day I returned to the window and noticed that the car was still standing in exactly the same place they had abandoned it. Then, to my surprise, it seemed to disappear when I wasn't looking. I hadn't heard anyone come to collect it and I didn't see who drove it away, but for some reason I just couldn't get those two young men out of my mind.

If anyone was to ask I couldn't honestly say why I left the twins at the park that night. I remember feeling unusually tired and thought that I would take a quick nap before I went to pick them up, but I didn't expect to remain asleep for as long as I did. And, to my intense disappointment, Peter fell asleep too. When I awoke I felt petrified. At first I turned over, trying to shake off whatever it was that I was dreaming about, but the screaming was so intense I could barely stand it. I fumbled around the floor, feeling for my glasses. Having fallen asleep on the sofa, I had obviously knocked them off and couldn't see a thing. I wasn't sure what was happening but suddenly I realised that I wasn't dreaming at all and felt horrified at what was happening around me. I was anxious to get up and felt myself panic as I tried to get up from the sofa. I was losing it and felt certain that I was going crazy again. My heart was pounding and I wanted to vomit; I had never felt so scared. The noise that penetrated my ears was so overwhelming that I could barely think. The beautiful home that I had closed my eyes on suddenly resembled a scene from a battlefield and I wondered what the hell had gone wrong. I repeatedly told myself, 'This cannot be happening.' But suddenly Peter's words struck and their meaning was clear. Although I felt disorientated, I tried to raise my head from the sofa, knowing by the urgency in his voice that every second counted. Peter screamed at me over and over again, 'For God's sake, Marie! Wake up, wake up! Run for your life, Marie, run! Please get up and get out of here!' I couldn't see him clearly, just his outline, but the unfamiliar sound of someone hacking on wood penetrated my ears and the screeching and yelling of someone in pain sounded so unfamiliar; yet I knew it was Peter. I leaned forward to gain my balance and almost managed to sit upright to grasp my glasses, when suddenly it happened. Everything became clear and with one stroke of his machete, the flesh on my arm was sliced raw and my terrible ordeal began. I couldn't believe what he was doing. I heard him call, 'You're my fucking wife! Get up, get up!' It took me a while to react to Smithy's demands, so he instantly flared into a violent rage. His hands were unsteady and trembled as he viciously prodded at my chest with the sharpened tip of the machete. I felt the blade penetrate my skin but was amazed when it didn't cut straight through me. How I managed to keep a grip of myself I don't know. I wanted to run and scream at the top of my voice to attract attention, but I knew if I had I would have been as good as dead. His voice was hard and callous and his face looked fierce. I had never seen him look so evil. My instincts told me to get up and run, but in that split second my contemplation of escaping seemed hopeless. I knew that he would kill me; all that he needed was a simple excuse. He was desperate and severely panicked at the thought of being caught, so I knew that he had a terrible fate planned for me. The more he panicked, the more he frightened me, but when I eventually managed to stand up he caught me off balance and I almost fell stomach first onto the blade and cried at the thought of what might have been. But his brutal threat to kill me there and then made me stop instantly. I felt so choked with fear and yet the thought of dying and leaving my children heartbroken was the worst feeling of all. I knew that in a situation like that

I couldn't allow myself to become hysterical and, for reasons I am not sure about, I looked him straight in the eye. I did everything he demanded of me and tried to remain calm. He didn't like to see women cry and had an unusual hatred for those who were sensitive, so I wasn't sure how he would react if I broke down. I felt the tip of the machete slice through my shorts as he lashed out at me, and I pulled away from him not really knowing how much pain he wanted to cause me.

I tried to calm him, but he was totally out of control and ordered me to lead the way out of the house. I turned to the right to leave the house via the back door, but he cornered me and prodded me to the left as he hurled abuse at me, then prodded me all the way up the stairs to the children's bedrooms and back down again. He was even more angry at not finding them in bed. 'I would have killed them if they'd have been in bed!' he said. Still prodding me, he forced me out of the front door. I couldn't stop myself from shaking and my heart was pounding so fast that I thought that my chest was going to explode. 'Move it, move it!' he yelled. 'I'm going to fucking kill you; I'm going to cut your fucking head off.' He glared at me like a mad man and I knew that he meant every word of it.

At that moment I was conscious of delaying every move that I made, hoping that he wouldn't realise, but he was well aware that since Peter had escaped from him it would only be a matter of time before the police were called. He swore he would find Peter and kill him too. Then he persevered in getting me out of the house and off the streets before the police had time to arrive, by which time I had panicked so much I was totally out of breath and could feel my pulse racing. The injury on my arm was beginning to throb and yet the flesh from my wound looked raw and lifeless. My blue denim shorts were soaked with my own blood and the very thought of losing too much terrified me. I felt my knees buckle as I began to feel faint; I was certain I was going to pass out.

Suddenly my attention was completely taken away from it when, in the corner of my eye I noticed Kizzy, our fluffy white Samoyed. She was the newest addition to our family and had done no harm to anyone. Totally unaware of what was happening, she came bounding through the back door, yapping excitedly. Then, to my horror, he took one clean swipe with the blade and almost caught her. Luckily she frolicked from one side of the road to the other and he missed her. I panicked in fear for her life and called at the top of my voice, 'Home! Kizzy, home!' My voice trembled but I prayed that it didn't sound too diverse for fear she wouldn't respond, but then she stopped and looked up at me. I think she sensed that I was in danger. She wouldn't go home; instead she reluctantly followed us, keeping as much distance between him and her as she could. She was a good little dog, intelligent enough to know when something was wrong. Suddenly, without warning, Smithy picked up a stone from the gutter and hurled it at her, hitting her hard on her side. She yelped uncontrollably and cowered helplessly, but she still wouldn't go back home. Instead she followed us all the way to the end of Hagnaby Road and round by the chicken sheds, but then stopped. That was the last I saw of her. By that time Smithy was so enraged he ordered me to move quickly and jump the narrow dyke which was situated between the chicken sheds and the cornfield. He prodded me with the machete, directing me to the right, bringing us back on ourselves and past the back of my house. Kizzy was nowhere to be seen but I could hear her barking frantically. Neither of us had ever ventured as far round as the chicken sheds before, so I guessed that she was feeling as frightened as I was. I was absolutely terrified and I knew that there was a possibility that by the time my ordeal was over, I may not see her again.

The continuing pain in my arm eventually took my mind off her and all the time I was being prodded and shoved around, I was trying to think of ways to escape him. The cornfields were desolate and I could hear no-one, it seemed like a lifetime before I eventually heard the faint cries of my children and the sound of sirens in the distance. It had been a long time since I had prayed, but on that night I prayed for what seemed like an eternity; not just for me but for Peter, my children and poor little Kizzy too. I kept on telling myself that it wasn't my time to die, but then I wondered if it was, who would love and care for my children? Then I asked myself; what if he went back and killed them all? My eyes filled with tears at the thought and yet I was so horrified I couldn't cry. The sound of the sirens told him that the police were a good distance away from us, so they didn't seem to worry him. 'They won't find you where I'm taking you; not alive anyway,' he snorted.

He found great pleasure in reciting every gruesome detail of his intended torture and killing, which he had so carefully planned out for me; even to the point of taking his own life if he thought there was a chance of getting caught and going to prison. He wasn't prepared for that.

The main devastation for me seemed to be the removal of my head and the disposal of it. I was not only afraid of dying, but repulsed by the way he had threatened to kill me. I trembled uncontrollably and found myself trying to change the mood he was in so that I might live longer. I said things to him that I wouldn't have said under normal circumstances and asked him, 'If you cut off my head, how will anyone know who I am?' He laughed hysterically, like someone totally insane, then automatically stopped like he wasn't amused at all. Then he poked and prodded at me like I was nothing, directing me over fields and dykes, forcing me further and further away from my home. I noticed that his intention was to forcibly guide me into the direction of Chris Cookson's place. Her husband, Gary, was the gamekeeper for those parts. I prayed that he would still be working and see me in the fields, but it just didn't happen.

I knew that once Smithy had forced me to the top of the hill to the bunker that he had spoken about, he would kill me and throw my head to the bottom, like he had threatened. It was at that point that I began to wonder how many other human parts he had thrown to the bottom of that dark hole. After all, he didn't originate from Old Bolingbroke, but he seemed to know the area pretty well for someone who had only visited once or twice. He had landmarks planned out on a map ready for his escape and held a whole lot of knowledge of the roads leading in and out of the place. I figured that he'd either really gone to town on making sure that he wouldn't get caught after killing me, or that he had done that kind of thing before. I wasn't sure which. All I knew was that he meant what he said; he would kill me. The fact that he had a car waiting for him, and knowing that it had stood outside our house for almost a day without anyone reporting it, told me that he was no amateur. The only hiccup that he admitted making was that he had allowed Peter Senior to escape and alert the police; that was his biggest regret.

I heard the police calling my name at the bottom of Hagnaby Road, but I couldn't understand for the life of me why they remained there. I felt like they were just waiting for me to appear in front of them, knowing that it wasn't going to happen. All kinds of strange thoughts went through my mind. Did they really want to find me or were they afraid of him too? I heard their dogs barking but they seemed so far away and travelling in the opposite direction, so I knew even the best sniffer dog wouldn't be able to pick up either of our scents. It seemed everything they did was all in vain.

It took Smithy only minutes to get me away from the house. So far away that no-one thought it possible to get that far on foot. In a short space of time we were well out of the expected radius and I didn't expect anyone to find me. Although I didn't understand why at that time, he ensured that I jumped across every available dyke that he had previously mapped out, sometimes forcing me over the same one more than once. He knew that the dogs would lose our scent in water. It was only when my ordeal was over and I was asked to relive the whole thing, in a bid to clarify my statement, that I was informed by the police that each time I had crossed the dyke my scent had been lost. So he had made it virtually impossible for their dogs to track me down. Smithy was well aware that they wouldn't find me. I remember cursing the police beneath my breath and asking myself, 'Why are they searching so close to my home when I'm so far away?' Then I realised if I wanted to live, it would be up to me to break free.

There was no-one there to help me and I knew at the time that he wasn't going to let me go, so I walked on and searched the ground for bricks, rocks, anything that I could risk picking up to hit him with. It was at that point that I noticed that our Lincolnshire fields were a consistency of soil and thick grey clay; nothing more than that. Then suddenly, there it was a single lump of stone. My feet hurt, they were sore and I pleaded with him to slow down, hoping that it would give me time to grab hold of the stone. But he didn't concern himself with the pain I was in. Why should he have? He was going to kill me anyway. He had abducted me from my home, barefoot, and had bellowed, 'You won't need shoes where you're going!' So I should have known better, but I thought anything was worth a try. I didn't want to die, so I tried to keep him talking so he wouldn't notice the large lump of stone that lay in our path but as I cautiously approached it, I looked over the land and thought to myself, 'Surely our world is far too beautiful a creation for there not be a God.' For the first time in a long time, I looked up to Him for help, knowing that I had long since disserted him; I pleaded with God to save me. It was at that point that I realised, if I was meant to die then it would happen anyway. Trusting in Gods' judgment, I felt myself relax as I approached the stone and casually stepped over it as if he was guiding me. I realised then that I wasn't in a position to battle with Smithy and was suddenly made aware of it. Somehow I just knew that it would be a risk that I couldn't afford to take.

I reluctantly spoke to Smithy and he seemed to respond quite well, but then he mentioned Carol and his temper flared up again. I suddenly wondered if it was all about her. "She told me"! He yelled at the top of his voice. "Who"? I asked. "Carol", he replied. "She told me all about it". Then it dawned on me. Her malicious tongue had been at work again and she had told him a distorted version of the truth of what I had said, when I had confided in her, where I had been and who I was with and, as he put it in his own words, 'advised him what to do about it.' I couldn't believe it; I was stuck for words. I had known her all my life and yet it still shocked the hell out me to be told that she had provoked him into doing such a thing. But I was quick-witted and replied in a very soft voice, "Well that's funny because it was her who told me that you didn't love me and that you didn't want me anymore; that's why I left you". For the first time since the beginning of my ordeal, he seemed to calm down and stopped in his tracks to glare at me.

Although the machete that he held in his hand was a good twenty-four inches long and three inches wide, his Rambo-type scarf and clothing seemed to be the main thing that I focussed on. It was only then that I realised whose character he had adopted. Rambo, he was dressed as Rambo. It seemed to me that he had convinced himself that he was actually Rambo.

I felt the terrible pain in my back and chest where he had been prodding me with the machete and wondered how much damage there was underneath my crop-topped T-shirt. For the first time since he had abducted me, I was able to take stock of the situation. His gaze was fixed on my face but expressionless, his ebony-coloured hair hung below the headdress that he wore and his slender physique was just as toned as it had always been; definitely a resemblance of Rambo. But I asked myself, 'Why the hell does he want to be like Rambo?' I had noticed that the machete was identical to the one that he had kept hidden in his drawer back at the bungalow, and the cloth that he usually wrapped it up in was tied around his neck like a scarf, and then I wondered how much more there was to this man than I already knew.

By following his very distinctive orders I had managed to stay alive and had jumped every water-filled dyke that he had ordered me to. He seemed to know where he was heading and led me to a much wider, deeper dyke further up the field. Although we had had weeks of beautiful sunshine, each side of the dyke was heavily bogged down with mud and I felt myself panic as I stood high up on the banking, looking down at the depth of the water. Just for a second I hesitated and told myself, 'It's going to be impossible for me to jump across that!' I had jumped the previous dykes on impulse, but that one was clearly much deeper and widespread, so I doubted my ability to jump across it. I wasn't quite sure how deep it was but I was afraid of getting bogged down in all the mud, so my hesitation prompted him to prod me in the small of my back with the tip of the machete. The very second I felt the sharpness of the point; I leapt forward just hoping that I had taken a wide enough leap to take me over to the other side. I felt my pulse pumping blood through my veins and the sound of my heart echoing all around me. It seemed like the whole world was spinning on an axle and I could barely breathe as I lay face down in all the mud where I had landed. Feeling very disorientated, I tried to raise myself up from the ground before he had a chance to follow me. Never before had I felt such agonising pain inside my stomach; I felt nauseous and almost vomited when I suddenly realised just how close I was to losing my life. Then

I heard him cry, 'Get up or I'll kill you!' I struggled to do as he said. I was weak and only able to raise my head far enough off the ground to see his face and witness the fierce look that he gave me. Then suddenly, without prior warning, he leapt forward intending to land where I was, but lost his balance and fell neck high into the water. As I stood up and looked across at him, I could see that he was shaken and struggling to free himself from the filthy water, mud and weeds. Just for a split second I felt inclined to help him but as soon as I had gotten over the shock, I realised that he was no longer in control of me and I felt the urge to run. As he struggled to free himself, he sank further down until his chin was level with the water yet he didn't seem to panic. His main concern seemed to be keeping the machete out of the water. As I gazed in amazement I focussed on the glimmering blaze of the blade as he held it high above his head as if to strike a pose to impress me. Although he was at risk from drowning, he wouldn't let go of that damn machete. It was then that I realised it was time for me to run and get out of there. I scrambled to the top of the banking as quickly as I could, leaving him to fight his way through the slime and weeds, and all the time wondering if he was behind me. I couldn't stop myself from shaking and my knees felt weak but somehow I still found the strength to pull myself together and I ran like a bat out of hell. I wasn't sure where I was running to. I don't recall thinking too much about it, only that I had to get as far away from him as I could.

I had no idea where I was, he had forced me to a part of Old Bolingbroke that I had never had cause to visit before so I just couldn't get my bearings. Yet my mind insisted that I should run for it. I heard the sound of my own voice echo inside my head, as I repeated the word, 'Run, run, run.' As I headed off across the field, I wondered how long it would take him to free himself from the weeds and get out of there. Then I found myself hoping that he would never get out of it alive. As I ran, I tried to avoid the thick thistle plants that stung my feet but there were so many of them it soon proved pointless and I found it easier just to endure the pain. My heart beat so fast it felt like I was carrying it in my throat; I could hardly stand and yet I just kept on running, knowing that if I didn't he would have killed me. I raced towards the edge of the field hoping I was heading in the right direction of the road, but it seemed so far away I began to wonder if I'd ever get home alive. I feared for my life and, as my legs buckled underneath me, I urged myself to keep on running. So I ran and I ran and I ran. I ran about the fields in hysterics, my heart thumping, fighting for breath when suddenly I realised that I was heading for a full blown panic attack. My head began to spin and my eyes clouded over and wouldn't focus. I was petrified. My breathing had gotten so fast I could barely draw in breath and the tingling sensation that I experienced began to creep up my limbs towards the top of my head, but to my astonishment I controlled it and became calm again. I needed to cry, but I knew if I had I would have panicked more and I might never have been able to control it. I knew that I had to remain strong to keep on going; I owed that to my children. Although I was exhausted, I just kept on running. Occasionally I looked back over my shoulder to see if he was there, but I never stopped running. I needed to rest but the very thought of being mutilated horrified me and the thought of such news being broken to my children really sickened me.

I couldn't believe what he had done... and all the time I wondered why.

I gazed across the land; what had once seemed to be a tiny village now felt gigantic. Although my mind was filled with doubt, I told myself, 'If you could only reach the road, you could run for help.' The road was more open, but I knew without restrictions I had a chance to get to the bottom where I had heard voices and the sound of dogs barking. Then suddenly from what seemed out of nowhere, a familiar part of the village came into focus and I began to cry. Tears of relief rolled down my cheeks as I told myself, 'For God's sake, Marie, run for it!' I took my last stride from the field onto the recently resurfaced road and cringed as my bare feet touched the warm tarmac. I felt the loose gravel cut into the soles of my feet; the pain was everlasting. I could see all the way down to Hagnaby Road where we lived, but to my shock and horror I couldn't see a soul. I could tell by the cool air that it was getting late and all I could think about was getting to my children before he did. He had told me back at the house that he would have killed them had he seen them; I needed to ensure that he didn't. It was a long stretch back down to Hagnaby Road, and I continually pleaded with God to keep my children safe until I got to them. It had been a long time since I had been able to move so swiftly without fitting, but I kept telling myself, 'Come on, Marie, you have to do this!' My fear of collapsing in a pile in the middle of the road was at the forefront of my mind, but I had hoped with all my heart that God would hear my prayers and give me the strength to see it through. I had never felt so anxious. I wondered if Smithy had been watching me and had reached Hagnaby Road before me; maybe he was waiting for me at the bottom. I was halfway down the hill before my knees began to buckle, the intense pressure caused me to overheat and suddenly I realised that I hadn't taken my Carbamazepine - just one more thing that I had to worry about. I had so many thoughts in so little time. It was as if I was up in the air looking down on myself, watching my whole life pass before me.

The life I had once resented so much suddenly felt so important to me and, like a gift from God, I was granted a second wind that helped me to run much faster. I ran so fast I almost toppled over. I couldn't believe that I had managed to get away without him following me. The soles of my feet were burning and I was in agony, yet I still managed to find the strength to run through it. Just before I had reached Hagnaby Road I panicked when I realised I had to turn the corner where I could not see, but impulsively I jumped over a garden fence to avoid it so I could seek help from a neighbour.

Taking no particular notice of the two black Labradors that tried to ward me off, I ran to the front door of the old farmhouse and entered the hallway without knocking. I spieled off everything that had happened that day to the people that I met inside. I felt so desperate I sought help from them even though I didn't know them. As I entered the house, I felt a terrible sadness and felt ashamed for invading their privacy. My arm was still bleeding so I tried to position it so that my flesh wasn't gaping, but I knew instantly when I set eyes upon the proprietress that she was disturbed by my presence. Following moments of hysteria, she called for help and was comforted by another female. The man of the house looked the typical gentleman farmer and instantly showed concern for me. Within seconds he had asked me an assortment of questions and caringly led me into a room that resembled a kind of banqueting hall. After trying to calm me down, he offered me a seat at the head of a long dining table and proceeded to unlock a gun cabinet which was facing me. I paid particular attention to the dog that had positioned itself by my side and sensed that it somehow knew I was hurt. When I looked up I saw three people - the proprietress, her daughter and the farmer - each showing concern. At that point I felt that I had been guided by God Himself and, just for that moment, I felt relieved. I felt a fluttering inside my stomach as the farmer ordered one dog to stay by my side and the other to follow him. As each dog positioned itself, I realised that I had spieled off enough for the whole family to appreciate that it was a matter of life and death. I warily watched their movements and hoped that I hadn't given them more than they could handle. I immediately felt remorseful for any danger I may have put them in and kept telling them so,but then I realised that they were better protected than I was. As the farmer hurriedly moved about the room, I noticed that he had removed what I thought to be a 12 bore shotgun from the gun cabinet and once again ordered one dog to remain by my side while the other accompanied him outside in a search for Smithy.

Even amidst the entire trauma, I felt an extraordinary absence inside that house. I instantly felt sorry for the mature woman and wondered why she had looked so sad. It seemed that no matter where I was or what I was doing, I constantly acquired the intuitive evaluation of others. I knew that my sudden appearance had made her feel uncomfortable but I felt sure that there was something more than that. Suddenly the opening of the front door disturbed my thoughts and took my attention away from her. I trembled with fear and my teeth were chattering; I was absolutely terrified. I expected Smithy to appear before me and hoped that the dog that sat next to me was as protective as it looked. Never before had I felt so relieved to see a man in uniform. 'Where are my children?' I asked. The very thought of them being hurt instantly made me cry. The room gradually filled up with officials and, for the first time since the beginning of my ordeal, I was able to cry and broke down; I cried so much that I felt sure that I would never stop. I couldn't bear the thought of my children being hurt and knew only too well that if Smithy had seen them before the police had, he would have killed them. The police officers assured me that my children were in their safe keeping and that we were all safe. I gazed at them through my tears and wondered if they really knew what it was like to come face-to-face with the likes of Smithy brandishing a twenty-four inch machete. I doubted it.

Smithy had purposely dressed as Rambo, and travelled seventeen miles from Skegness to the secluded village of Old Bolingbroke with a lethal weapon and the intent to kill. I knew we couldn't possibly be safe until they had apprehended him and he was locked behind bars. The man was a psychopath and needed treatment. I knew that and so did they.

Suddenly I had so many people around me; it was difficult to see who was doing what. I felt the weight of a blanket wrapped around my shoulders and wondered how it had got there. There seemed to be so many people asking me questions, yet so little done to get me out of there. I wasn't thinking rationally and nothing that anyone said seemed to register or even make sense, then I recall being helped from my seat and slowly coaxed into going back outside, aided by the ambulance staff. Then, to my dismay, there they all were - those who I thought could have helped more had I been important enough. At that moment I felt totally let down by the Lincolnshire police force, who took a wild guess that the 999 call that they had received that night wasn't serious enough to warrant mechanical aids or extra staff. Lots of doubts went through my mind at that time and I trusted no-one. I climbed into the back of the ambulance which stood outside the front door of the farmhouse and I realised that none of us were as safe as we perhaps thought we were. I remembered telling the Magistrate earlier that year what kind of a person Smithy was, but he didn't believe me. I was horrified to think that I had to endure all of that before I could prove that my word was good and I wondered: would they believe me now?

—◊◊◊—

A Place of Safety..?

I sat down opposite Peter Senior. 'How come you're still here? Why have they not taken you to hospital before now?' I asked with hostility in my voice. I felt no sympathy for him; in fact I felt quite bitter towards him. All that I could remember was that he had abandoned me when I needed him the most. Surely he must have realised that I could have died in that house, being left alone with Smithy like that. He showed me no more compassion than I was showing him. I wasn't sure if it was shock or simply that we blamed each other for what had happened. Then I saw tears rolling down his cheeks once he had realised that it was all over. I lowered my head in shame as I realised at that particular moment, it was difficult for either of us to sympathise with anyone.

A twenty minute ride to the Pilgrim Hospital seemed to take forever and all I wanted to do was sleep, yet I felt so on edge I daren't even close my eyes. I had been told that the police were escorting us to the hospital, but at that stage I didn't have a lot of faith in them and wondered if we would be safe even then. I wasn't pleased with their decision to allow Carol to transport my children to the hospital and then wait with them at the reception, knowing that Smithy was still at large. In fact, I was really angry at the thought of her being informed of the attack at all, but it seemed that so many arrangements had been made in my absence that I wondered if anyone had expected me to survive my ordeal. I felt that I had no choice but to fall in line with the arrangements that had been made during the time of my abduction. After all, I had never been in that situation before, so I wasn't quite sure how things worked.

My arm began to pulsate even though the ambulance staff had applied an adhesive dressing; I began to think that it was too tight. Then I remember wondering how the hospital staff would remove it without tearing my flesh further apart and without hurting me. I tried hard not to think about it but for the larger part of the journey that's all I could think about. I wasn't sure who was more nervous, me or Peter Senior. Although he remained silent, I could see that he was distressed and yet I still didn't feel for him. It seemed strange that someone I had felt so close to just hours before, now felt like a total stranger. In the back of my mind I was continually trying to work out who was responsible for what had happened - was it me, Carol, Peter Senior, or did Smithy carry this out single- handedly? I didn't think so! Although there wasn't any doubt that he was the one who had abducted me and attacked us, it was difficult for me to believe that he had planned it all by himself. As soon as we had arrived at the hospital, we were taken through to the casualty department where it seemed we were waiting for hours. My arm was still pulsating and I was still worried about the removal of the dressing.

I wondered where my children were as no-one had informed me of their whereabouts and it felt as if I was just being left in the dark. To a certain extent I thought that everyone who had become involved was treating me more like the assailant rather than the victim. At that particular time I had not been informed of any arrangements that had been made regarding alternative accommodation for me or my family, and at times it felt like the police signified I might have been to blame for the whole thing. Then, when I was advised not to return to Old Bolingbroke, I was devastated. For the first time in a long time I cried and found it easier to let my tears flow. The children loved Old Bolingbroke and I felt totally responsible for taking away the only thing that really made them happy. After numerous questions the police made it clear to me that they had struggled to find us shelter and, unless they succeeded in apprehending him, he might strike again. Part of me felt that I should have returned to Old Bolingbroke as I was made to feel guilty for putting everyone to so much trouble. But then I realised, had my application for a Protection Order not been dismissed earlier that year, this might not have happened at all.

The person who showed me most respect that night was the physician who stitched my wound. I recall him being very tall, well built and black. The very thought of being stitched petrified me but he was so gentle that I felt really comfortable with it. I looked away while he cleaned and examined it, and nervously watched over him as he injected the raw flesh several times with anaesthetic. I said nothing more to him than, 'How on earth are you going to put all that flesh back together?'

He pulled up a stool, sat down beside me and smiled, then wittily replied, 'Just like this.' And, taking hold of my arm, he began to stitch my wound. He made me feel so relaxed and had so much natural empathy that I wondered if he was as gentle with all his patients. I don't recall how long it took him to stitch my wound, but I remember it didn't feel half as bad as I thought it was going to.

I lost track of the time and was eager to know how my children were. It seemed the more relaxed I was, the more emotional I became and found it really difficult to hold back my tears. I suffered flashbacks and remembered many things that had happened during the day and weeks before, and still I couldn't help considering the possibility that someone else may have been involved in it all. My mind drifted back in time thinking about all the things that could have been done to prevent it from happening, but then I told myself, 'Maybe he would have done it anyway.'

Peter Senior sat quietly in the same cubicle a little further up from me. He hadn't said much all night. As I glanced across at him, I saw a lot of dried blood around the back of his head and shoulders and noticed that he had several knife wounds to his back, all oozing with blood. And yet he waited patiently until it was his turn to be stitched. There didn't seem to be an immediate rush to attend to him and I wondered why. It was only at that moment that I began to feel sorry for him. I hadn't realised how bad his injuries were up until that point. I sat there looking across at him, remembering how Smithy had viciously hacked away at first his head and then his shoulders, intent on killing him. He had been lucky to get away alive. I had no idea what he was thinking, and then I suddenly thought, 'Maybe he thinks I'm to blame.'

It had been a very long night and my children had been waiting in the accident and emergency room for hours and had fallen asleep on the benches. Carol had waited alongside them. 'We's been 'ere all fuckin' nite!' she said in her aggressive slang. From the moment I saw her she never stopped complaining. I particularly remember her sarcasm as she nodded over at Peter Senior and said, 'T'way he carried on o'er phone, I thought Smithy 'ad fuckin' killed ya.' She spoke indistinctly hoping that I wouldn't hear her but, being partially deaf, I think she said it a little louder than she anticipated so I immediately picked up on it. 'What! Is this not gruesome enough for you, Carol?' I asked. Once she had realised that I had heard her, she turned and walked away from us then tried to look sympathetic. It was one of those nights when her sarcasm hurt more than usual and I hadn't been prepared for it. I don't know why I let it bother me; it was no more than I expected from her. She was first rate at kicking me when I was down, so why I expected her to be different that night I don't know. I was thirty-eight years old and still struggled to understand what it was that made her so malicious. We had always been different I knew that, but I couldn't for the life of me understand why she was so unsympathetic and deliberately unhelpful when she expected so much from other people. I had always done my best for her and had never asked her to pay me back what she owed, yet she still hated me. Sometimes she was frightening. Her behaviour was somewhat unusual and, although I didn't know much about manic jealousy, what I did know seemed to give an adequate description of her typical behaviour and I wondered if that was the reason why my family made excuses for her.

I was very apprehensive about leaving the hospital that night. I had been made aware that Smithy was still at large and felt very uneasy. My children came away traumatised and I was in no shape to care for them, but it was apparent that no-one else was willing to either. I wrapped my arms around the twins, as I nervously walked along the corridor and, when they looked up at me for reassurance, I managed to raise a rather bogus smile when all I wanted to do was cry. Carol spieled off everything that had happened that night again and again, knowing that it worried us. She spoke vaguely of a place of safety that the police had arranged for us. I couldn't think what possessed them to tell her so much when they knew so little about her. After all, I don't recall anyone in authority speaking to me regarding protection for myself or my children. I felt like we had been cast aside and that was the end of it.

The days that followed were worse than any I had ever experienced; nothing seemed to go right. We travelled to Grantham, where I understood the police had promised us a 'safe house' but when we arrived there, there wasn't one. So we spent all night walking about the grounds of Grantham Police Station trying to make sense of what had happened. There were no facilities made available to us and no refreshments offered. The children hadn't eaten since tea-time and I was desperate for a cup of tea, but it was a long, drawn out night with very little progress made. It seemed that no-one was expecting us so we were continually asked by police staff why we had been sent there and each one of us in turn explained the best way we could. We were shown very little consideration and were passed from pillar to post throughout the whole night. I couldn't believe the police operated that way and thanked my lucky stars that I didn't have to rely on them often. I don't remember exactly how long we were there for, but I remember sitting on a small wooden bench, cooped up in a tiny room known as the waiting area. Each one of us took it in turns to sit down as there wasn't room for everyone. Feeling very frustrated, I almost made the decision to go back home when a constable called me to the desk and explained, 'A gentleman from the South Kesteven District Council will meet you at 49 Bridge End Road in the morning.'

Meanwhile we hung around until daybreak when we were passed over to Grantham Victim Support team, who kindly found us a place to stay so that we could take a bath and catch up with a few hours' sleep. We had no clothing to change into, no food or cash to buy any with, and everything we owned had been left behind. I had no idea how we were going to cope, but by that stage I didn't much care.

The twins cried constantly and wondered why their whole world had been tipped upside down. We had lived in Old Bolingbroke for almost eight years - the largest part of their lives. They didn't know anything else so they were heartbroken.

Despite my objections, Ian had chosen to remain in Old Bolingbroke. He was angry and had no intention on being shanghaied to another part of the country. He had been attending Boston College since he had left Spilsby High school, and had made friends. He had settled in his work and was doing really well, so he was adamant that he wouldn't allow anything to spoil his career. Like me, Ian was a little too reserved at times so he found it difficult to make friends as a youngster and, because of my unsettled way of life; he suffered at the hands of other children and wasn't as readily accepted in some areas as he should have been. But he was a good kid and I feared for him. He didn't understand how dangerous Smithy was and, although I tried to persuade him to come with us, he just wouldn't. Brian volunteered to take care of him and, because I trusted him, I agreed but I never stopped worrying about him. I took a huge risk that night, although I doubted my decision. Ian was so responsible I trusted him and once again put my faith in God. After all, it was Ian's life and at the age of eighteen he was the one who had to decide. I knew that.

Although I did what I thought was right that night, I wasn't thinking rationally and there was no-one there to advise me so I did the best I could in one of the worst situations I had ever been in. The following day we met the gentleman from South Kesteven District Council and were given the keys to a two bedroomed terraced house, which he labelled, 'a safe house'. I felt like a fish out of water. I was miles away from home in a town that I didn't even know and for hours I sat motionless in one of the worn-out chairs that had been left in the middle of the front room. The house felt cold and uninviting and I had no idea what I was supposed to do. My life had come to a standstill but what really hurt was that no-one showed concern. It was at that moment that I realised, apart from Carol tagging along for the ride, we had absolutely no one to turn to.

Peter Senior was fifteen years my senior and had suffered five lacerations to both his head and back. Some of them had been overlooked and hadn't been stitched at all, but the two deeper ones at the back of his head had been stapled and caused him so much pain he had to take pain relief every four hours. He wasn't a young man and I could see that the attack had taken its toll; he was in no condition to comfort anyone. I felt the warmth of my tears as they trickled down my cheeks and I wondered how we were going to get through it. My children had been through so much and it seemed that no matter what I did, I just couldn't get it right. I wondered if they would be better off without me. I felt isolated. None of us dared to leave the house and, had I not taken the initiative to phone the Lincolnshire Social Services Department, none of us would have eaten. A few days in that house felt like weeks. As we huddled together behind locked doors, we tried to re-establish exactly what had happened to us and why. It seemed that everyone, apart from Carol, had suffered shock and felt a need to release the terrible fear that they carried inside of them. What one couldn't remember, the other could and I found trying to cope with all the fear that was projected from first one of us, then the other, just as alarming as my own recollection of the abduction.

During the moments of despair, my determination to survive helped me to cope and yet once it was all over, the constant reminder of what might have been really horrified me. The constant flashbacks and distorted images of Smithy brandishing that machete was far more than I could bear, and at times I could have sworn that I was going crazy. Although I repeatedly begged Carol not to talk about it in front of the children, I felt she purposely emphasised every gory detail knowing that it frightened them. Her description of his machete was strangely accurate and yet, to my recollection, she hadn't been there to see it. I spent many hours studying her emotions, wondering how she knew almost as much as I did. Although we were miles away from Old Bolingbroke, I still felt uneasy and even more so with her there. I recall she spent most of her time sitting in the front room observing every car that passed by the front window. I couldn't relax around her and I couldn't sleep at night; I found it impossible to be in close proximity to her. I was petrified and all I could think about was the phone call that Carol had made to me before Smithy had attacked us, the strange cars that had parked outside our house the day before, and Smithy himself. I remembered at that point that the police hadn't been to check on us and no other support had been offered. While Smithy was at large, we were left to pick up the pieces and put our lives on hold until he had been apprehended. It seemed that the arrest of just one man took precedence over our welfare, simply because the Lincolnshire authorities had not got sufficient resources to cater for such a crisis. I was so disheartened; I felt that I had been let down by everyone.

I had no idea what I was supposed to do next. My children were not attending school and still none of us had clean clothes to change into. There were only three beds in the house to sleep five of us, and only a few bits of crockery. There were a couple of items of furniture that looked as if they had been discarded and no curtains to hang up at the windows. All in all, we were destitute. By the time the police had arrived to take statements I was in a terrible mess, my nerves were in shreds and my injuries had swollen and become bruised. My feet had almost doubled in size and the pain was so excruciating

I could barely walk. For some strange reason the police didn't show any sympathy; and I noticed that they ran through our statements in a matter of fact way. I was the first one to make a statement then Carol made one after me and, although she had openly spoken for days about the time leading up to the incident, I got the impression that she was reluctant to co-operate fully with the police. I wasn't allowed in the same room while she made her statement so I didn't hear anything that she had to say, but my intuition told me that she wasn't prepared to give a true and complete account of the occurrences that had taken place between her and Smithy. Just hours before the police arrived, she had tried to make excuses why she should leave before they got there. For the duration of her stay I felt a strong sense of disloyalty and deceit and had a strong suspicion that she only remained with us so that she could make things right for him. Despite being asked to keep her own counsel regarding our whereabouts, she carelessly made a personal telephone call to Steve, the landlord of the Cherry Tree, knowing that she was jeopardising our safety. Many times she had openly declared that she had seen Smithy drive past the 'safe house' and gave an accurate description of the car I had seen outside my house in Old Bolingbroke a little before he had abducted me. I felt really anxious as I knew there was no way that she could have described that car without having seen it there first. I believed that she knew far more than she admitted too and there was no doubt in my mind that she was protecting him. It was strange how her persona changed once the police had arrived. Her voice no longer sounded insensitive and she was far more composed than she had been, but I suspected that was in an attempt to gain their immediate approval. I never once took my eyes off her while she remained in the room and each time she spoke; I wondered if the police would have the insight to detect her deceit. Somehow I doubted it.

All of my life I had been trying to get to the bottom of her character, yet still even up to that point I was no wiser than I had been as a small child. Some of the things that she had said to me made no sense and the more she spieled off, the more mysterious she made things sound. I believed that she did that kind of thing purposely to cause uncertainty. I had no doubt that she was toying with me, psychological games had always been her thing, but when she involved my children I became very angry and found it impossible to remain calm around her. I don't think I had ever despised her as much as I did then. I recall I wouldn't leave the room for fear of her following me and yet I didn't feel that it was safe to leave the children alone with her either. The terrifying thoughts that she placed into their minds were not normal and I told her so. I thought it was strange how she spent much of her time trying to convince us that she was as frightened of Smithy as we were, when she had previously spoken about him like he was a martyr then in contradiction claimed to wonder why he had done such a thing. She knew as well as I did that he was capable of doing anything. I believed he would have killed me in an instant.

There was an intense atmosphere that night. The police left the 'safe house' with our statements and we each recalled what we had said. Carol was very evasive about the contents of her statement but proclaimed that she had 'done her best'. I felt sick to my stomach when she finally confessed that she had told them that she knew very little about what had happened. I felt sure that she had concealed a lot of what she did know in a bid to protect him. However, Peter Senior and I spoke openly for hours then came to the conclusion that it was far better not to trust her, as she was probably as deceitful as Smithy himself. She had never once sympathised with us and, while we struggled to stretch our food out to feed her, ourselves and the children, she smoked cigarettes continuously then pleaded poverty when I begged her to loan me money to help restock the food cupboard. She had always been selfish at the best of times but when I realised how much money she carried around with her, I was disgusted. For three whole days she had watched us suffer, even eaten alongside us after we had been aided by the welfare. She took food from my children's mouths when she had enough funds to feed us all for well over a week. It was an accident that I saw how much she carried in her purse, but the moment I did I felt justifiably hurt. I knew her well enough to know that she was hard-hearted but it had never occurred to me that she would sit back and watch my children starve rather than help us.

I thought it unusual for the police to keep her statement secret and even more so when they refused to divulge what either of us had written. At that point I wasn't sure who my enemy was and who was my friend. I had been let down by the police so many times in the past that I felt I couldn't even trust them; I had never felt so alone.

The police took their time in arranging for photographs to be taken of our injuries and assumed it would be better for us to attend Grantham Police Station rather than they come out to us, yet they had seen how painful it was for me to walk. They had already seen the damage caused by my being abducted barefoot, but still arrangements were made over my head and I had to fit in the best way I could. Carol drove me to the police station and I wasn't surprised when I saw her jotting down her fuel expenses so that she could bill me for it later; there was no charitable side to Carol. By the time the week was through, I owed her an absolute fortune, but I gave no thought to ask her to make deductions for the food that she had robbed us of. It had never occurred to me until then why she so willingly appeared during a crisis, but then I realised that she recorded absolutely everything so that when it was all over she could present me with a bill for twice as much. She even accepted weekly payments when I struggled to pay it. She preyed on people like me and made a good living doing so... uhh! I sigh! Even today she has not changed, but it is only now that I realise that she is not the fool. I am.

I spent five long days in that house worrying about our future; I had never felt so helpless. I felt terrified at night and feared the daybreak and yet I remained strong for the sake of my children. The days when I would have packed my bags and walked out of there were behind me and I felt well and truly trapped. I recall I had once found it easy to run away from circumstances like that, but I found it difficult to run and hide while I was caring for the twins. I no longer had the strength to chase dreams like I used to. There was no perfect world waiting for me just around the corner and no Prince Charming to bail me out. Although it was difficult for me to accept, that was all I had.

In a world that was constantly changing, I found picking up the pieces difficult. People were not as ready to help as they used to be and I found the constant battles between myself and the local authorities totally devastating. I had never found it easy to beg, not even as a child, but when I arrived in Grantham I was forced to put aside my pride and humbly grovel in order to gain my entitlements. There was very little consideration shown to people like me. Children like mine were expected to join the thousands of others and roam the streets, but I knew we deserved better than that. I hadn't struggled through life to join a society of outcasts, so I battled with the authorities and earned myself a reputation for being painfully persistent.

For six months I tried to get our lives back on track, during this time Smithy had been arrested and charged, but I felt because of his families' status he got away with a far lesser charge and was later sentenced to 18 months imprisonment for grievous bodily harm instead of attempted murder. The twins had more than their fair share of problems in and out of school. And by December 1997 our lives had practically crumbled. I had really gone downhill and my doctor had referred me to Carroll, a counsellor from the Grantham Resource Centre. She was the kind of person I thought I would never need. It was then that I first tried to tell my story of 'Little Molly', not because I felt I had to but because I wanted to. In my heart of hearts I knew I needed to begin somewhere but, as much as I wanted to, I just could not confide in her. I was so messed up I couldn't remember where I had come from or where I wanted to be and, apart from Peter Senior, I trusted no-one. Carroll shared my thoughts for almost a year but she still didn't know me. Despite her professionalism, she barely touched the surface of my troubles and I knew before

I left her that within a few months I would be back trying to tell my story to someone different.

In a period of two years we moved house three times in and around Grantham and each time it was following incidents that involved my sister Carol. Although she had returned to Skegness where she lived, she maintained contact with us by regularly inviting herself to our house and convinced us that Smithy was aware of our whereabouts. It was always a mystery how? Finally I came to the conclusion that she was our biggest threat and we would only be safe if I turned my back on her. Once I realised that, I cut myself off from her completely but she never gave up. Although we moved from house to house without informing her, she spent a lot of her spare time tracking us down, and reappeared on my doorstep with her daughter, Wendy, just to let us know that she could. She amused herself by it but I didn't find it so funny.

—ɯ—

CHAPTER 15

On the Move Again

By August 1998 we had been given three different homes by Kesteven District Council in and around Grantham. None of them were adequate but we made do. Then suddenly things became serious, when yet again Carol was the bearer of bad news and informed us that Smithy was serving a shorter prison sentence than he had been originally given and was being released to an address in Grantham. I doubted her word at first but then I saw a grave look appear on her face that told me more than her words could ever say. Then I knew she had finally succeeded in disrupting our lives again. I felt really angry and just didn't know what to do next.

The house that we lived in was more beneficial for the children's needs and, although we suffered psychologically, we had settled there. The twins had made a few friends, and Ian had joined us and was doing fine. Although he had to leave college, he had found himself a job and worked full time, he had made lots of friends, passed his driving test and had bought himself a car; something he had always wanted to do. I felt so proud of him. Despite all our difficulties, he was the one who held it all together and fared quite well. He seemed to grow up really fast and never let things worry him; either that or he hid it really well. I'm not quite sure which.

After seeking help from my practitioner, I was re-referred to Carroll, the counsellor at Beaconfield again. In turn, she referred me to 'Mind,' a charitable organisation who had previously helped people like me. I was embarrassed at first and refused to go, but then I realised I really needed them. The name 'Mind' carried a bit of a stigma, but without them I was nothing. I wasn't even a victim any more. I was just Rosemarie Smith from nowhere. Suddenly I had become one of those mysterious people who walked the streets of Grantham looking totally absent-minded. Following yet another bout of depression, I approached the organization not knowing what the future held for us. I had never visited a place like that before so I was nervous and found it difficult to converse with anyone, but the staff coaxed me into trusting them. Although 'Mind' was situated in the centre of Grantham, it seemed so peaceful there and I felt more relaxed than I had done in months. The staff seemed to know how I was feeling and handled our situation with care. I felt really safe there. It was a place where I was respected and equal to any other person I spoke to. At last I had found an organisation I could rely on. Instead of wandering around Grantham worrying about Smithy, I was able to unload my troubles onto someone else's shoulders and, within no time at all, my problems had been halved. I must have met the most thoughtful person in Grantham that week. Although I was initially unaware of her status, she later informed me that she was a semi-retired magistrate who used her authority to help those who were in need. Although she couldn't divulge when

Smithy was going to be released from prison, she agreed that it would be best for us to leave Grantham.

I couldn't believe that Smithy was being released from prison so early. We had spent over a year going through so much torment. It was a life worse than hell and the children had suffered so many traumas that it showed in everything that they did, but still we battled on hoping that one day they would pull through. I found it unbelievable that the authorities had allowed him to be bailed out so close to us, especially as they had not warned us about it first. He had hurt so many of us and had ruined so much of our lives, and yet on his release the government fed him, clothed him and helped to aid him back into our society. I found it almost unbelievable that the very same people who were supposed to be protecting us were protecting him; the only difference was he was a higher priority. He had almost killed us and yet, in the eyes of the law, his need was greater than ours. He had served around eighteen months in prison - only half of the sentence he had been issued with - then walked free, receiving aid from the government. He indisputably fared better than we did. It seemed that the support he had received was not sought but given to him as an automatic right as an ex-offender. I couldn't believe that all that was allowed to happen, and underneath our very noses. I don't know what made him attack us that night, and I dare say that I will never know, but what I do know is something needs to be done about our system.

Monday, 24th August 1998, was the day that we finally left Grantham. I had spent the whole weekend packing while I watched the children take their bedrooms apart and become emotional about moving house one more time. I hated living at Grantham and

I think the children knew that, so at that time a new house was accepted more readily than it had been in the past. We hadn't been able to view it and we had no idea where Market Deeping was, but as I knew I had no choice I signed for the tenancy on arrival; a five-year-old semi. It was instantly obvious to me that the property didn't belong to South Kesteven District Council, as it was exceptionally clean and very well maintained. They had only been too pleased to refer me as I had been a thorn in their sides ever since I had arrived in Grantham. At that point I became Longhurst Housing Association's responsibility.

I stepped down from the removal van feeling very apprehensive and took a slow walk towards the front door of the new house. It was open and I could hear women's voices coming from inside. Before I had a chance to knock, I was greeted by a Longhurst housing officer and the existing tenant. They were polite and exceptionally well spoken. After introducing themselves, they invited me inside and I could see instantly that in comparison with the South Kesteven District Council properties, it was faultless. As I viewed the house I instantly noticed in addition to it was built a large conservatory and I was asked to sign a separate document accepting ownership of it. That was to safeguard Longhurst taking responsibility for any repairs that it may have needed in the future. At first I was reluctant, but when I was advised that it would be dismantled if I didn't, I willingly signed. I liked it and had noticed that without it the house would have proven too small for my family. When the women left, I inspected everything in the house. I didn't like the size of it; it was unusually small and caused me to feel very claustrophobic, but I guessed it was better than being in the same town as Smithy. Within a few minutes there was a knock at the door and a workman named Geoff appeared. He spoke politely and explained that he had been sent by Longhurst to carry out a few essential repairs to the property. It was quite a while before I realised that he was actually stripping the conservatory of its electricity supply, and then I became angry. Yet again it seemed that the authorities were taking liberties. I was the new owner of the conservatory, but only when it suited them. After I had given it some thought, I realised that I was in a position to compel them to re-install the supply… and that's what I did. Apart from that, the day went well. I was really pleased with the time it took us to move in. Needless to say, I had noticed that the locals weren't as considerate or as helpful as I had expected them to be, as they stood and gaped inquisitively while we struggled to unload our furniture from the back end of the van and never offered so much as a cup of tea. I remember hoping that they were just a little reserved and not actually disagreeable to our sudden appearance, but it soon became apparent within the days that followed that we were not welcome.

When we finally settled in, I eventually managed to get Allishia enrolled into 'The Deepings Comprehensive School' and Kyle continued to attend 'The William Henry Smith School' for boys in Brigg West Yorkshire. Ian had met his girlfriend, Sam, and lived in a flat on the outskirts of Grantham, while Cheniel remained with Nigel, coming home only at weekends when everyone else was there. That left me on my own most of the time. It was strange really, because once I had come to terms with living at Grantham I had spent most of my time roaming the streets like every other outcast. But when I arrived in Market Deeping I hid myself away more, like a recluse. I took care of the children when they were at home but, when I was left alone, I remained in the house were nobody could see me and continually fretted over Smithys presence. I didn't consider Grantham far enough away to keep him at bay and I kept on wondering why the authorities had been so negligent in allowing him to move into the same area that we were residing in, knowing of the terrible circumstances. After all, neither of us had originated from Grantham and there were so many other councils that they could have nominated us to; it just didn't make sense. I couldn't believe that the authorities had allowed this to happen. It seemed as though history was repeating itself. I was the victim, yet I was treated no different to the assailant. Even though it felt like the world around me had been crushed, I was just expected to pick up the pieces and move on.

—⁓—

ᘓᕬ CHAPTER 16 ᕬᘓ

A Cry for the Victims

Before Smithy was taken to court, I was advised by the investigating officer to claim compensation for the injuries that he had caused me. But I remembered even as a young girl I had been deprived of the Government award that most child abuse victims had received, so I knew that if I wasn't prepared to seek legal advice and once again do battle with the authorities, I might as well forget compensation too. I was horrified to think that we had suffered all that we had and yet it was so easily forgotten. The authorities had more or less discarded us, as though they had simply thrown us in a pile like a piece of dirt, and it was that which made me want to fight for compensation.

Compensation didn't come as an automatic right in the way that the police investigating officer had led us to believe; we had to fight for it tooth and nail. It seemed that no-one was prepared to do anything for us without gaining something in return and I felt really bitter about that. I knew I had to fight for my rights, but the most difficult thing was listing the reasons why I thought I deserved compensation, as if my statement had not been specific enough.

At a time like that even the innocent are made to feel guilty and it's almost impossible to know who the guilty one is. Although I didn't want to believe that I was responsible for Smithy's actions, I thanked my lucky stars that the final decision wasn't actually mine but lay with the judge who had been assigned to cross-examine me.

I had never appeared before a Judge to claim compensation before and, although I was extremely nervous, I was convinced that the Judge would understand that it wasn't a matter of 'how much' but consideration for the person who stood before him. I had hoped that he would not only see that I was a young mother fighting for her rights, but also fighting for something to believe in. I needed to know that there was at least one person out there looking out for us; I needed to know that we were safe.

I was one of many that stood in the High Court waiting area that day and, like the majority of people, my face didn't fit. I didn't speak with the Judge as I had expected... I was tried by him. Although he was aware that I was suffering from severe anxiety depression, he gave me no more consideration than the next person. He made it clear that he did not sympathize with me and seemed more than satisfied to blame me for provoking Smithy in to doing what he did. After asking to see my scars, he decided that the £2500 that had already been offered to me was far too much and reduced it by half. 'Consider it as a gift from the taxpayer,' he said. While those words rang through my head, I remained silent, thinking about all the anguish we had suffered. I recall I was stunned.

It was the first time that that Judge had laid eyes on me and yet within minutes he had categorized me and made it very clear that he did not like me. I left the courtroom feeling ashamed; the guilt came later. I wondered if it had all really been worth the anxiety it had caused us. Then I realised that the whole charade was just a process that the authorities put you through just to make you feel better. But I didn't feel better. I didn't even consider the £1233 nearly enough for the shame and embarrassment that I had to endure inside that courtroom.

A whole lot of emotions went through my head while I stood inside that courtroom. It was almost as if the Judge had agreed with what Smithy had done and even gave specific reasons why he thought he had carried out such an attack, blaming my cohabitation with Peter Senior. He did not take into account that I had previously approached a solicitor to begin divorce proceedings way before I had met Peter Senior (the fact that the law disallowed it until I had been married for a year was neither here nor there). And even though the courts had previously awarded me ineffective protection orders in a bid to protect me and my children from him, it seemed that he condoned Smithy's wrongdoing. I felt astounded by his remarks and couldn't understand how he had progressed to become a Judge; surely it was his duty to punish the assailant, not the victim. I understood only too well that on occasions people were discriminated against, but I hadn't expected it within the courtroom. Yet again I felt let down by the system and I didn't feel that justice had been done. When I returned home, I was so ashamed I felt too embarrassed to discuss any part of the hearing with anyone so I never mentioned that day again.

I remember that Judge's words with such clarity and still despise the fact that he was far less than caring, but I suppose in a way he helped me to understand more of why people like Smithy do the things they do. I never really recovered from the shock of going to court or the damage that was caused by my trying to make amends for something I had been convinced was my fault. I believed what my counsellor told me, that time would heal and I would be able to move on with my life; what I didn't realise was how long it would take me.

—∽—

CHAPTER 17

Once an Outsider,
Always an Outsider

Before I knew it, it was December 1998, I was aged forty and my life seemed to be no better than it had been when I was just fourteen. I had struggled all of my life and there had been times when I was so convinced that I wouldn't even make it that far. I had never really been sure whether that was my own fault or someone else's, but as no-one had ever taken responsibility for the abuse that I had suffered all of my life I took everything upon my own shoulders, creating more intensive work for my counsellor. I still hadn't made up my mind about psychology and, although I had been re-referred to Carroll, I still wasn't convinced that she was the right person to get to the bottom of my troubled mind.

I found it difficult to settle in Market Deeping. It was a strange place where the wealthy resided on one side of the town and the less fortunate were housed by the local authority on the other side, in an area known to the locals as 'no man's land' as far away from the centre of town as possible.

For almost four months I had been waking up to the sound of the early morning traffic rushing past my window and the awful sight of identical housing structures that surrounded my home. Already the view had become tiresome and I was feeling caged. I really hated it there but with nowhere else to go I gave it my all, thinking that I might get used to it. But after I had been living there for six months or more, I found that many things tainted the town and what I saw on the surface was nothing compared to what was hidden underneath. The true locals seemed very protective of their own town yet didn't give a lot of thought to anyone in need of a friend. Outsiders, who were fortunate enough to afford property of their choosing, lived in the more idyllic areas of the town and snubbed council tenants like myself. Up to that point of my life I had never lived south of the Midlands, yet I had heard so much about it so I rather expected it to be different to what it was. Given time, I learned so much about the town that I renamed it, 'The Town From Hell' and did as the others did judging everyone on looks alone and speaking to no-one. I struggled to survive in Market Deeping as I had always relied on people being kind to make me feel at home, but it seemed the more I put myself out the worse I was thought of. Within the first year I noticed only the strongest survived. The weak gave up on themselves and entered into an anomalous world they felt safe in, or took their own lives. The river which ran through the middle of the town seemed to give solitude to those who were burdened with the grief and anxiety they incurred from others. My life was such that I felt smothered by a cloud of loneliness, and it came as no surprise to learn that many living within the Deepings area suffered greatly from a depression that hung over them for many years.

When I first arrived there, I thought it was the escalating violence and systematic street fighting that caused me to loathe the place, then I realised that was only a small part of it. I can scarcely remember how many times I had to phone the police to try and prevent gangs from forming on our streets, but there were never enough police on duty to attend a situation and fights broke out anyway. The locals were so acquainted with the procedure, they laid money down that the police wouldn't arrive and many innocent people suffered for it. I watched families come and go because the townsfolk wouldn't accept them, yet I had seen many stay knowing that they were going to have a tough time of it. At first I wondered why they had stayed, then I realised that some found it easier to stay rather than move on as their lives before were actually worse than what they had to put up with here. And, like me, they felt trapped.

I have lived amongst many types of people during my life, but I can honestly say that none were as fear-provoking as some of the people I was unfortunate enough to meet at Market Deeping. Although I had lived a life such as I had, I found the behaviour of many disturbing and sometimes got the impression that they were far from normal. I could never understand why they attacked each other on sight, sometimes to the extent of unconsciousness and so close to death before they were willing to back away from each other. Some people around there suggested that interbreeding had caused the violence in them, but they had no proof of that. When I first arrived there, I was informed by a local that if I wasn't a fighter before I arrived I would be before I left. I guess that was true, not only for me but my children too. For years they defended themselves and took the blame for others so that they would fit in, but now they realise they are outsiders and will never fit in. What the locals didn't realise about me is that I had always been a fighter, not so much physically but mentally I was strong and I'm sure it was only because of that I survived. Where others submitted to their weaknesses I remained strong, although I do remember there were times when even I was beaten, but I got up fighting and still live to tell the story. Others were not so lucky.

When I first arrived there I found it difficult to believe that the police didn't always respond to the 999 calls that people made, then I witnessed it for myself and saw the damage that was caused by it. It was only then that I understood what the root of the problem was. I couldn't just blame the people. I had heard so many police officers maintain that there was a low crime rate in Market Deeping, knowing as well as I that there was a serious problem there. But for them to accept it didn't help the property market. I wondered at the time how they could remain so nonchalant when people were being injured and torn apart. They were aware of the townsfolk running riot at the mere sight of an outsider and those who were weaker than themselves, but a lot of the time they did nothing about it. It was a tough thing for me to come to terms with, but it took me no time at all to work out that each officer that lived around Deeping had property at stake and that seemed to be the main reason why they thoughtlessly bestowed a false reputation on the town, putting not only mine but other people's lives in danger.

Dave was the first police officer that I came into contact with. He came across as a rather jovial sort, quick witted yet rather slovenly, but then there was a part of him that I just couldn't understand. He wasn't what I called a typical officer on the beat and I found that when I had the need to approach him. He casually dismissed anything I had to report and dealt with crime in such a way that those who were regularly offending were left to simply re-offend again. It wasn't his fault, I knew that. He was one of the youngest officers around Market Deeping at that time and only followed in the footsteps of the more senior ranking officers, who simply sat at their desks giving orders to officers like Dave. Basically they ordered him to jump and he jumped. So long as he didn't rock the boat too much, they allowed him to plod along nicely.

Occasionally he had cause to call on me regarding my son, Kyle, who at that time wanted to be just like 'Rocky Balboa' and had been seen fighting his way through a ferocious gang of locals. Yet the only information that Dave held was where Kyle had been defending himself. Although he came away with telltale injuries, he just couldn't prove that it was the locals who had commenced fighting. I originally thought that it was just boys being boys, then I realised that there was more of a pattern to the enmity that the locals displayed and every Friday and Saturday night alike, some kid suffered a harrowing attack similar to that which Kyle suffered each time he crossed into the Deepings territory. That's when I became worried. Although Kyle was only eleven years old at the time, he wasn't a lad to be reckoned with. Having special needs and all, he didn't think like other boys and I knew that within a certain period of time, if the police didn't protect him from the locals then they would find themselves in a position where they would have to protect the locals from him.

None of my children had lived an easy life and, although I had heard many people say that they had had a better life than most, it didn't compensate for all the hard times they had experienced. I knew that I had let them down but even so I battled on and tried to do the best I could, hoping that one day we would walk away from there with our heads held high.

At times it felt like I was dwindling backwards. Frightened to accept how much the locals pushed me to my limit, I struggled with simple tasks. Listening to my inner self I knew that I was failing, but then I asked myself, 'How am I supposed to free my son from his inner rage when I have bought him to a town ruled by inner tyranny?' I was uncertain. I had expected so much when we first arrived there, freedom of the town, our rights and privileges; but I was traumatically disappointed when we were robbed of all three.

CHAPTER 18

The Aftermath of Child Abuse

I couldn't believe what was happening. I had already suffered one breakdown and was terrified of suffering another. It hadn't been easy the first time around when the twins were only babies, but at the age of eleven they were old enough to be as frightened as I was.

That morning my mind was all over the place. I wondered how my children would cope and who would take care of them if I couldn't hold it all together. As tears streamed down my face, I realised that my cheeks and my fingers were numb. I tried to remain calm but Allishia stood by my side and clung to me and wouldn't let go. I heard her call my name over and over again; until the sound of her voice faded so much that it disappeared into the distance. The bellowing inside my head got so loud I just couldn't bear the sound. I tugged at my hair hoping to bring back a normal sense of feeling but the numbness travelled down my face until it reached my toes and gradually took hold of me as I panicked. I rubbed vigorously at my head hoping to put an end to the strange sensations that terrified me so. Then came the fear of the unknown and I stumbled to the floor as I desperately tried to move forward. Sensing nothing but panic, my palpitating heart beat faster than it ever had before as the fear I felt inside seemingly pounded at the walls of my chest. I fought for breath as I struggled to maintain consciousness, but then the huge black cloud at the end of the tunnel, followed by the aura of bright light, seemingly tempted me.

I had lost all sense of direction and felt that there was nothing to keep me in a world that I had learned to hate so much, but just for a single moment I visualised my children all alone. I needed to remain strong I knew that. Suddenly I was in darkness and struggled to breathe, but the will of this thing was too strong for me and I collapsed on the stairs motionless.

Over the years that followed I lost the ability to function and, although I could see and understand, I lost the ability to communicate, giving me moments to study others and learn to understand them.

When I finally met Clive Powell, I learned that I could only move forward if I let go of the past and tried to focus on the future, but trying to do so at that stage was impossible. I had entered an anomalous world where I felt safe. The depression had burrowed itself so deep into my soul that it destroyed every single thought that I had.

I lay awake in my bed wondering how I had got there; the room was dark and the house was still. No sound of my children to break the silence. For a few moments I was able to enjoy the state of waking without the fear and flashing images that taunted my brain. For a short while the feeling of terror inside my head was almost bearable. I gasped for breath as terrifying thoughts entered my mind as I glanced over the heavy duvet that covered me. Unable to escape whatever it was that was taunting me, I lay paralysed by fear. Certain that my life was almost over, I cried but my tears did not flow like they used to; I slept but dreamt only of the terrible life that I had lived before it. I could not see a way out.

I had been living at Market Deeping for almost two years before Doctor Wilson referred me to Clive. It was only then that I began to look at everything that had happened to me.

I had never experienced true happiness and, because I blamed myself for many things which had happened during my life, I had always felt sad and lonely and that sorrow seemed to rub off me onto my children. I had always blamed myself for being abused and constantly allowed it to plague my mind during adulthood, so I spent most of my time fretting over something that I couldn't change and considered myself a far lesser person than anyone else. My mind was so full of past emotions that it left little room for rational thinking. But when I met Clive, he counselled and worked alongside me and gradually opened up a whole new world for me.

I recall the day I arrived at one of my later sessions; I was feeling very much out of sorts. My life had slowly got out of control again and I was feeling worthless. After spending countless years in the dark hidden away from everything that I feared, I looked upon the face I had come to trust and slowly unloaded a whole range of troubles, trusting he would guide me through them. As I sat on the couch opposite him, I noticed what seemed to be the only object in the room that day. A dreary black and grey abstract painting, a strange work of art that looked dull and lifeless, it seemingly had the power to make me feel more sombre than I had ever felt before. Leaning against the wall of the conservatory, its hellish colours seemed to bellow out at me as I reluctantly glanced across at it. As my thoughts suddenly changed direction, I listened carefully to Clive's voice while he gave me a synopsis of the painting. Paying particular attention to the shapes and colours, I saw a hint of midnight blue with many different shades of greens and browns. All in all it looked a devil of a painting but nevertheless I couldn't take my eyes off it. When he asked me to describe what I saw, I gave him a quick summary and asked who had painted it. I had already convinced myself that he could not have painted such an awful painting, but as he so cleverly avoided my question I just smiled and changed the subject so that I didn't offend him. Nothing more was mentioned about the painting until a few weeks later during my next session, when I saw a more beautiful abstract painting standing in its place. 'You have a new painting,' I remarked. As I admired its colouring, I noticed that there were patterns and shapes that I couldn't identify and yet it was so beautiful, the vibrancy of colour was so strong it seemingly brightened the whole room and made me think of summer. I really liked it. I liked the way the artist had mingled the assorted pinks and purples and the bright red, orange and yellows that made me feel warm inside. It made everything seem bright and beautiful. I sat back and relaxed in my seat as I admired it. After revealing my thoughts, I said, 'I'd love to be able to paint like that.' 'You could,' he promptly replied. Clive was an optimist through and through and I suppose that helped me to have a little more confidence in myself; he believed in me and convinced me that I could do anything. Suddenly I caught him smiling, as he casually announced that the painting was in fact the same painting that I had seen a few weeks before during my previous session. I couldn't believe it. The painting had not been moved or altered and yet it looked so different. I must admit I wondered if he was just testing me, but then I realised the painting had not changed; only my thoughts had. After all the years of counselling I had suddenly noticed that when I was happy I looked at things differently, so no longer saw the painting as dull and lifeless. Instead the colours had seemingly sprung to life and the beauty of the painting enthralled me. It took me a while to realise that out of an innocent evaluation of an abstract painting, Clive had not only been able to analyse my thinking but had helped me to understand that life was very much like a painting. During times of anxiousness my life seemed dull and lifeless, but of course it was far more beautiful than I cared to admit. I learned many things from that session; how different the world looked when I was feeling sad and lonely and how quickly life around me changed when I looked at life positively.

I recall telling Clive one day how much I wished I could have seen myself from the eyes of those who had previously judged me. 'Something else to write about in your journal,' he said. I had written many things in my journals before I eventually wrote my first book 'Little Molly'. But the most recent thing that I was able to unload from my mind was a significant verse that I scribbled down on my notepad while remembering my awful past. Having been abused as a child I carry many emotional scars, but now Clive has helped me to find a way to release those inner fears and I have learned to simply let go.

Ernest is one of the many poems I have written since I first started writing and, although I sometimes wonder where it is all going to end, I keep on writing and moving forward.

Ernest

Ernest is not an imaginary friend;
he is not a sound or a scene.

He's in every little girl's conscience;
he's a moment, a nightmare, a dream.

He cannot be described or forgotten,
he exists in any shape or form,

In a little girl's memory as a demon.
No date to which he was born.

He may appear all tongue-tied and twisted;
he may appear merry or forlorn.

He may appear and rest on one's shoulders,
in the evening, afternoon or dawn.

He is neither man, beast or structure,
of heights impossible to impose.

In every little girl's conscience, Ernest
preys where fear grows.

Perched on the slide in a playpark,
on a swing or a sledge in the snow,

Why does he exist on such ruin? I would
beg him; take leave and let go.

But he, who has no reason to comply;
for he will gain no reward,

If only I could reason with Ernest,
I would have no fear at all.

—ɷ—

No doubt many of you are wondering why I have written such a strange poem. Was it solely because I was disappointed in all the people who had judged me unfairly throughout my life or a pitiful self-evaluation? But it was neither.

When I was a young child I used to wonder what would happen if Ernest ever caught up with me. Would he come and take me away like my siblings said? Did he have spikes on his head and look like a demon, like I was told? How fast could he move, would he punish me for wetting the bed or making too much noise? The minute I heard my siblings call out 'Molly, run! It's Ernest!" I thought there were only minutes to spare, so I ran and I kept on running. Fearful for my life, I searched for somewhere to hide and panicked at the thought of being caught by him. There was no-one there to protect me so I lived in constant fear of him.

I was a small child growing up with the fear of Ernest always on my mind. To me he was more than just a man who regularly wore a plaster cast on his foot or his leg and struggled to walk as he passed our house. He was a nightmare; a dream I couldn't wake up from. He was the Bogie man that I went on to fear all of my life.

It's difficult to understand the damage one can cause by telling a child that Ernest is coming, or the ten o'clock horses are coming. It's only when I think back to my own childhood that I realise that our greatest fear either comes from someone playing a practical joke on us or something which is drummed into our heads as children.

A cruel word from my siblings was just the beginning... but the fear and torment lasted forever.

It's quite strange really as I have always found writing poetry difficult and I have never felt that I was good at it, and yet from the very moment that I was able to write I would scribble the occasional verse such as this onto sheets of paper. I suppose it was like everything else really, it didn't seem important but words just fell into place and eventually a verse would appear in front of me.

I remember there were many times when I had wished with all my heart that I could have changed occurrences, things that I had kept to myself. Then I placed my trust in Clive. If only I could have turned the clocks back. After many years of practice, I thought I had learned not to dwell on the past or what might have been and yet I was constantly plagued with heartbreaking memories.

When I remember my past I think of some of the terrible things that even I have done and I know, whatever the duration of my life, I will never forgive myself.

When I finally plucked up the courage to talk to Clive, I spoke about my baby I had mourned for almost twenty years.

I began by confessing and told him, 'I have this recurring dream and in my dream I am nursing my baby. I feel happy, I hear a faint cry and yet I cannot see my baby's face.' As tears streamed down my face, I found it almost impossible to continue; grief gave way to despair and I had to pause and begin again. 'I was almost twenty-three weeks pregnant and didn't know which way to turn. I had been ill for some time and the twins hadn't even reached their first birthday, so when I approached one of the leading gynaecologists at Kings Mill Hospital in Sutton-in-Ashfield, I told him that I had concerns about having another baby and reeled off a whole lot of reasons why I thought I shouldn't keep it. Then I begged him to help me. I was so confused I didn't really know what I wanted and couldn't comprehend what he meant when he informed me that he could perform what he termed as, "an arranged miscarriage". I didn't know what the procedure entailed but I was convinced that it was the best for all concerned: my husband, Paul, me and the children. But I was so wrong. It was the worst thing I had ever done.'

I could not put into words how distraught I felt when I had to witness my baby being born and taken away in a bedpan. It was so inhumane!

I have never forgotten what happened that day and have never been able to forgive myself for allowing it to happen. I still grieve for my baby and continually ask myself, 'What on earth possessed me to do it?'

I cry silently as I pointlessly wonder whether it was a boy or a girl and desperately hope for the sake of my baby that somewhere out there, there is a heaven.

As I sit quietly at my desk I ponder for a while, while I wonder what it was that prevented me from leaving an oppressive town like Market Deeping. Now that my children have grown and I face an age of determination, I wonder if the same entity that kept me there now prevents me from writing. For I have lived through so much heartache and pain that I feel a strong sense of restraint as I try to rekindle former emotions.

My biggest fear as always is that I would lose my mind and the only memory that I would be left with would be insufficient to expound the truth with all fairness. But, surprisingly enough, I go on remembering the awful things that happened there and for those who did not survive I try to give a true and honest account of what I considered to be some of the worst things that I had ever had cause to witness.

I will never forget Cathy for as long as I live. A fun-loving girl with the friendliest nature, and yet she had been given a reputation by some unfeeling locals that was most unfitting. At the age of twenty-eight the world was her oyster, but with no-one to guide her she struggled and achieved very little. For years I had seen her wander past my window looking half the woman she could have been, and yet at times I envied her. She was a free spirit, young and hopeful, someone whom I admired, yet she was destined not to survive. It sometimes felt good to hear her throw parties; it didn't happen around there often but when it did it was usually her who led the way. I remember thinking 'the world would be a much brighter place if there had been more people like her around'. And yet, I believe that many would have doubted that, I'm sure. She wasn't born to my generation but she was someone that I liked; someone I am sure I could have related too. Reminding me of my own youth, she was occasionally unsure of herself, defensive, uptight.

I find it extremely distressing to recall the night I last saw her. It had been a quiet night yet I couldn't help thinking that it was unusual for that time of year. I had been dozing while relaxing in front of the television, when suddenly I realised that it was December 6th, 2008 and soon to be another year. At 10.45pm I was ready for bed and gave so little thought to life outside our four walls. I worried, as I did every year, about purchasing a turkey and wondered if I would be well enough to see Christmas through without having to attend the accident and emergency unit at Peterborough Hospital. And as always it was the right time of year to wonder where all those years had gone. Suddenly I was startled by what I could only describe as an uproar and horrendous noise which broke the silence, a terrible disturbance characterized by noise and confusion. I instantly felt nauseous and emotionally distressed as my body trembled from head to foot, the symptoms of yet another unsettled night at Market Deeping and an early indication that something terrible was about to happen. Yet even after trying to survive amongst the ungovernable souls who played havoc around there, I had not foreseen yet another suicide. A woman in love and so close to Christmas; I could not comprehend her reasons. I asked myself, 'In that frame of mind, would I not have considered my only child first or would the anxiety of raising a child alone only add to the burden of living?' For those of you who have never crossed that fine line, it is the darker side of hell that cries out the loudest when we are at our lowest, and the faint cries of our children become lost within the unconventional world that only exists inside a turbulent mind, causing nothing but havoc in a world we all at times take for granted. Cathy was no exception. Her life had proven to be tough at times, yet still there were moments when she was full of the joys of spring and her face radiated the true love that she held for her son. It was at times like that that people could relate to her, but on the night she orchestrated her suicide, she was alone. Oblivious to all her pain she put herself through the most horrendous ordeal and regretfully died in hospital just a few hours later. I refused to believe that it was an easy option for her as some people implied. How could hanging by the neck and suffering like that be an easy option for anyone? Once she had made her mind up, there simply was no turning back. Although it was said she cried out for help and desperately tried to free herself, no-one was there to help her.

I shed many tears for Cathy and the little boy that she left behind. Forgetting how things were around there, I thought it was one of the saddest things that had ever happened but then I realised that the saddest thing was not the taking of her life but the fact that no-one seemed to care.

It was no surprise to see all her friends proceed with their usual social gatherings and typical Christmas celebrations, as I had already observed that many of them where unfazed by her sudden death and only displayed a deep mourning as they passed her house.

I was only her neighbour but I was absolutely devastated by it all and felt genuinely saddened at the thought of never seeing her again. At one stage I thought my mind was playing tricks on me, as I could have sworn that I heard the same drumming noise coming from her house that I had heard on the night she had died, but her house had been empty for weeks and I wasn't sure that I believed in spirits of the dead.

Time seemed to stand still for a while as I came to terms with a young mother's death; it was more difficult than I had ever imagined. When my parents died I was so hurt by it that I never thought I was ever going to get over it, but I slowly convinced myself that it was their true time and life had to go on. With one so young, I seemed to find it more difficult to come to terms with.

The very thought of her little boy growing up without her grieved me deeply. Although the tears that I shed seemed to relieve me, somehow I couldn't stop thinking about him.

I was wrong to make the assumption that Longhurst Housing Association would have trouble allocating the house where she had lived to someone else just because a tragic thing like that had happened there.

It had only been a matter of weeks when a young local couple signed for the tenancy and were seen peering out of the windows, happy in the thought that her house now belonged to them. I had forgotten how terribly invidious these people were. Psychologically they had no morals; what was good, bad, right or wrong made no difference to them. Even the penetrating sound of the gigantic fireworks that they set off to celebrate their arrival showed their lack of respect for others, but at the same time put a clear message across that it was just unfortunate that a few weeks before a young mother from this community felt the need to take her own life.

Life was so unjust at times and yet I constantly told myself that I should be grateful. Cathy's life passed so quickly and the flowers that I laid in remembrance of her shamefully outlived her memory. Her existence was soon forgotten in and around the town where she had lived her whole life, and her mother grieves for the fact that she will never see her again.

For the duration of time I had lived at Market Deeping I had promised myself that I would leave, but ten years passed by and I saw the arrival of yet another year. January 18th, 2009 and I felt a strange sense of comfort knowing that I was unique to the people who lived there. Looking back over the road I have travelled, I am certain that had it not been for those I would sooner forget, I would not appreciate the good in others. Although I was certain that there was a particular purpose for my being at Market Deeping, I knew I would leave when the time was right.

When I was young I used to dream all day long about my future and what I was going to become. For some reason I thought by some unexpected means I would automatically become successful and live my life in luxury, but after a very difficult time I realised that life just didn't work that way and the only dreams that I have now are for my children. I try not to worry about them but subconsciously I grieve.

For reasons only Cheniel could rightfully express, she moved away from there and immigrated to New Zealand, for which I am so proud of her. Yet still I worry and I miss her.

I worry for Kyle and Allishia, who still at times find it difficult to face up to their responsibilities and still believe that they are paying the price for being born to me.

Then there is my eldest son, Ian, who - like me - constantly worries about everything but consciously hides it so that he can protect the ones that he loves.

All this and more I worry over. As I look back over my life I clearly see what mistakes I have made and all too often regret some of the things I have done. Yet a lesson that I have learned is I must keep moving forward into the future; it is that which matters not the past.

—w—

CHAPTER 19

A Reunion that was
Long Overdue

Saturday, 24th January, 2009 I suddenly felt an overwhelming desire to contact old friends, fearful of never seeing them again. I wandered over to the computer room and pulled up a chair, then began to tap away at the keyboard of the latest Dell. Inexperienced, I made a lot of mistakes and became very frustrated at the thought of not knowing how to use it correctly, then suddenly - though it seemed to come from nowhere - the small amount of knowledge that I held of Facebook seemed to increase and I found myself manipulating Windows to my own advantage. Within no time at all I had succeeded in locating the address of Arch Simpson, an ex-partner who I had lived with for almost two years. I paused for a while to allow my heart to stop racing and wondered if it was the right moment to send him the message I was longing to send. It had been so long since I last saw him, yet even after twenty-five years I still hadn't got over him. I glanced at his name for some time before I read aloud the message that I had discreetly composed and, before I knew it, I had clicked the mouse and the message had been sent. The thought of hearing from him again gave me a wonderfully warm feeling and the flutter of excitement that I felt inside my stomach was as breathtaking as it had been all those years ago. Even so, I wasn't sure that I had done the right thing. I had never stopped loving him and, even though he was Cheniel's biological father, I knew that she couldn't possibly remember him so I had more to think about than just my own feelings. I hadn't really given much thought to what kind of response I might get from him. Although I was pretty certain that it was the Arch Simpson that I once knew, I was also aware that people change with time and I wasn't sure that his response would be a positive one. Being the impulsive type, I hadn't really given much thought to him rejecting me but in retrospect I am most certain that had I considered our last encounter I most certainly would have shied away from it.

I left the computer room with a strong sense of aspiration; something told me that it was the right time to take a good look at my life, which left me feeling a need to rekindle some of the more pleasurable phases of my life when I had felt really happy. Although I sometimes found it difficult to accept that I hadn't always made the best of things, I recalled some of the happiest moments of my life and regretted walking out on him all over again.

For the rest of that day I went about the house doing what was expected of me and the following day I morally obliged when my son telephoned and asked me to go to their home and babysit my adorable grandchildren. It wasn't late and because it was an unusual request, I found an exceptional amount of pleasure in it which completely took my mind away from Arch and the terrible frustration that had overcome me in trying to master the art of our modern technology.

At 3pm I returned home rather exhausted. Although I had been longing to hear from Arch, I held back my curiosity for a while longer, then at 10:30pm I made my way back to the computer room, not really expecting to hear from him. I had always believed that all events were pre-determined; no matter what we did, we were powerless to change our destinies. But I had been wrong before and it seemed that I was wrong again. As I anxiously logged into Facebook, I paid particular attention to the icon which informed me that I had received one new message. A slight movement of the cursor disclosed a very short message which read, 'Hello Marie, what a lovely surprise. Yes, you're quite right; it has been a long time. Telephone me tomorrow (Monday) between 10am and 2pm, looking forward to hearing from you, Arch.' I was mesmerized. I couldn't bring myself to touch the cursor for fear I deleted it before I had made a note of his telephone number. I read the message over and over again; I had never felt so happy. I sat quietly for a moment, remembering all the good times we had had together. Trying to work out all possibilities, I stopped myself from dreaming when I realised just how many years we had been apart. I fumbled about the desk for a pen and quickly wrote down his telephone number, knowing then that I wouldn't forget it then I reluctantly deleted everything from the screen.

I didn't feel that I needed to hide anything, but during the years I had lived with Peter Senior I had found it easier to keep things to myself. After all, our relationship had been totally different to the many I had experienced before it and I wasn't sure how he would react if I had informed him. Peter and I had been together for almost thirteen years and still I didn't really know him. We had never discussed Arch, so I knew I wasn't about to start after all those years.

When I looked back over my life, I sometimes felt cheated. I had rejected the heart of the first man that I ever truly loved, simply because I didn't know how to be loved by anyone. When I first met Arch I had been through hell and back. I had no idea what love was and felt absolutely certain that no-one in their right mind would genuinely care for someone like me. I was almost 24 years old and had suffered so much abuse that I felt typically ill-fated and blamed all the wrong people for the way I felt. I couldn't comprehend all the love and kindness that he lavished upon me, or the elation that I felt when I was with him. But when I eventually realised that I loved him, I got scared and, when Cheniel was conceived, I feared entrapment so panicked and ran. I knew with two children I couldn't run from one place to another the minute I felt threatened. He was my love and my life but my brother, John, had discovered where I lived and made his presence known, so for the sake of safety and freedom I gave up everything.

I couldn't wait for Monday morning to arrive. I tried to keep busy hoping it would take my mind off of Arch, but whatever I did my mind was firmly fixed on making that call. I tried to think of things I might say to him and tried to envisage what I thought was most likely to happen after we had spoken. It had been so long and yet I felt totally seduced by the whole thing. Willing to do almost anything to rekindle what we once had, I waited patiently for Monday morning to arrive and, just as the clock in the hall struck 11:30am, I picked up the telephone and made that call. Once again he made a good impression on me and I was totally agreeable when he suggested that we meet. He didn't give me a reason why he wanted to see me and I didn't feel that I needed one, the arrangements just seemed to slot into place while we reminded each other of past times and old acquaintances. We agreed to meet like it was the most natural thing in the world. I noticed the tone of his voice had changed slightly and, although he tried to remain poised, I got the distinct feeling that he was just as eager to see me again as I was him. I agreed to meet with him on Tuesday 3rd February, not realising how difficult it would be for me to keep my word. I hadn't told him how ill I had been during the time of my breakdown or that I had been hindered with agoraphobia for the last decade. Instead, I simply agreed to travel miles away to meet the man I hadn't seen for twenty-five years. I agreed to all the arrangements without even thinking how I was going to get there; the more I thought about him, the more I wanted to see him. It had been a long time since I had held his hand or laughed with him and, while I knew it was once all over, I just knew from the way we spoke that there was still something there to rekindle. Just for that moment I felt good, I had no room for negative thoughts and knew whatever it was that he was willing to share with me, I wanted it more than anything. Then it hit me and I began to panic. I hadn't thought about travelling to and from Stamford where we had planned to meet and the sudden realisation of having to leave the house was more than I could bare. Then it was like all hell had been let loose inside my head and I began to worry myself senseless. I knew if I had to rely solely on my own capabilities, I would never have got there.

Stamford was only a few miles away from my home but it might as well have been a thousand, as I was certain that I hadn't got the confidence to travel either distance.

When Tuesday finally arrived, it took me hours to prepare. The weather had taken a turn for the worse and the roads were thick with snow. Part of me was hoping it wouldn't stand in his way but then I heard the sound of a text arrive on my mobile phone; I sensed it was a message from him. Although I continually assured myself that everything would turn out fine, I felt really sad and let down when I realised that he wasn't coming. It had been twenty-five years and I knew that I couldn't be any more certain of his motive for wanting to see me than he was mine, but I was so desperate to see him again. I anxiously waited around the house willing him to contact me. I thought long and hard about the way I felt about him and suddenly realised that it was a blessing in disguise that he hadn't been able to come that day, as just days later I received a telephone call from him suggesting that we meet the following Tuesday at a destination more local to me, a place I knew well, a place I had more chance of arriving at. For a whole week I tried to prepare myself for the hundred and fifty yard journey to the Towngate Inn where we had agreed to meet. That alone proved to be more unnerving than I had anticipated and at one stage I almost cancelled our arrangements. But I knew if I wanted to see him again I had to keep to the plans that we had made. In the meantime, just chatting to him over the telephone seemed to compensate for not seeing him that first day and gave me enough confidence to make that all-important journey to the Towngate Inn the following week. I waited in anticipation trying to imagine what it would be like to see him again after all that time. I had just celebrated my fiftieth birthday, yet suddenly I felt so much younger than that. I found myself willing the days to pass more quickly and felt a strange sense of independence as I honestly thought that my life could only get better. Finally realising what it was that I had been feeling for all those years, I knew my heart would always belong to him. Chatting with him over the telephone felt so natural. All the years that we had spent apart seemed to diminish into thin air and once again my life seemed very much a part of his.

The years had taken its toll and I was much older by far. My hair had turned white and my olive-coloured skin displayed many imperfections; all in all I was ripe with age and yet still I remembered everything about him. He was so sweet I could almost taste the good in him, yet as I suffered pitifully from the long-term effects of child abuse I never felt loved by him or even knew what it was exactly that he liked about me. For a whole week I did nothing but recall memories of the past, places we had visited and people we once knew, but not for a single moment did I ever remember having doubts about him. For years I had loved this man and yet I had never been able to understand those feelings. Now I was certain that my feelings would never change no matter how long I lived; I knew that I would always love him. It had taken me a large part of my life time to realise what love really was and, although I always knew that me and Arch had something very special, I hadn't up to that point learned what those special feelings were. I was nervous of seeing him again and, although I had tried to prepare myself for the worst, I had hoped with all my heart that if ever he did love me, he would love me still.

Tuesday, 10 February, I awoke feeling bright and cheerful - unusual but it was a big day for me and I was so looking forward to seeing him. I couldn't believe that the time had finally arrived for me to walk through my front door to meet the first man that I had ever truly loved; he was all I could think about. As I quickly showered, I trembled in anticipation of seeing him. Not for a moment did it ever occur to me that he may not come. Despite it having snowed heavily again, I felt certain that he would. The way that we laughed and excitedly spoke over the telephone, I just knew we were destined to meet again.

I rushed around the house while I was dressing and tried desperately to perfect my hair, yet only lightly applied my make-up. That was unusual for me, generally I would have applied more but I hadn't forgotten how he had once accepted me for who I was and I suppose I knew he would again. I longed for everything to be as it once was; I wanted to feel natural and unobtrusive so that he would fall in love with me all over again. I kept a close watch on the time and listened anxiously to our old grandmother clock as it struck 10am, then I realised it was an hour closer to my seeing him again, but still that old clock could not beat fast enough. At 10:45 am I began to panic, not for the fact that I was going out alone as I thought I would but with the fear of being late; that seemed to override everything. I slipped on my boots and grabbed my coat and, just for that moment, I thought of nothing but him and making my way to the Towngate Inn in plenty of time to meet him there. Astonishingly, I made it up there on my own without fretting or panicking - the first time I had been out of the house alone for the best part of twelve years. I was amazed that I was able to go it alone without becoming confused and disorientated, an affliction caused by fear. All those years I had sought refuge behind closed doors and wished for my life to pass more quickly, yet suddenly I felt reborn. I hadn't ever expected to see him again, not even in passing, as I knew only too well that our lives had been so different and the paths that we once followed could not have been any further apart. But my world had been turned upside down and I had been granted what I had been wishing for, for almost twenty-five years.

The ground was thick with snow. Although I was well aware of the elements and what could happen, for the first time in my life I trusted my instincts and knew that he would not let me down. When I arrived outside the Towngate Inn, my heart was beating so fast that I could barely breathe and the apprehension that I felt was the worst that I had ever felt in my life. I felt absolutely certain that he would come and yet, until he arrived I constantly worried that he wouldn't. With every car that passed I glanced anxiously at its driver, wondering if after all those years apart I would recognise him. I suppose I still expected the person that I last encountered; strangely enough I hadn't been able to think of him in any other way. I had been in love with his memory for over twenty-five years, yet suddenly as I stood cold and alone, I felt an overwhelming sense of panic as I feared I may no longer know him.

Certain that he was late; I slowly began to resign myself to the fact that he may not come after all. I was certain that he said 11am but already it was 11:10am, he hadn't phoned to cancel and I hadn't received a text so I stood on the corner of the street almost in tears, wondering what I would do if he didn't show. A large lump formed in the back of my throat as I struggled to see past that particular moment, then suddenly my heart lifted as a torrent of jubilation burst through me. Such pleasant warmth radiated my soul as my eyes caught sight of him. He had not changed, his smile and pleasant features were the same as they had always been and I could instantly see that he was the man I had fallen in love with. I smiled at him as he drove towards me, then anxiously stepped back to allow him access to the car park. At that moment I couldn't think of anything but the love I felt for him. Never had I felt such warmth and happiness; up to that very moment, I had never felt so complete.

In the past I had heard so many couples proclaim their love for each other and speak openly of their interpretation of the meaning, but I had always been sceptical. Until I had met Arch, I had no conception of the word, but then I become overwhelmed with a form of emotion I could not understand. I realised that I was feeling exactly the same way as I had back then. In the past I had always played safe with no regard to my feelings, but suddenly my thoughts and feelings spiralled out of control. Although I still felt a general need to protect myself from my inner feelings, I felt such intense emotion that I couldn't. My love for him influenced everything - my thoughts, my feelings, everything I spoke about and everything I dreamt about. Although I was certain we only had a few minutes, I wanted him to know that even after twenty-five years, I still loved him. I knew from that very moment that my feelings had not changed. I still loved him but no longer feared it or shut it out; instead, I embraced it for all it was worth. This man was my life and I knew with what little time I had

left on this earth I wanted to spend it with him. I had
lived many years in hope of that day and felt certain that
my life would be nothing without him. I had never felt so
happy. Although he wasn't aware of it, I loved him
dearly and felt a desperate need to be with him.

He pulled his car to a halt and I slowly walked
towards it, not really knowing what to say except
'Hello.' Words seemed to fail me as I felt a sudden
shyness and embarrassment at the thought of my love for
him looking obvious. It seemed very much like our first
date and, just as it had done back then, my heart beat so
fast that I trembled at the thought of being alone with
him. As I carelessly fumbled my way into his car he
quickly apologised for not being more attentive. I was
a little surprised by his lack of consideration; in the past
I had always known him to be considerately helpful and
courteous. Just for a moment I felt myself shy away from
him. But his fascination that my dark brown hair was
now astonishingly white gave us a focal point and helped
me to adapt to his company. Suddenly my overall
confidence took me by surprise and I smiled when
I realised that he was complimenting me. It seemed that
my attractive features had done it again. Although at
times I felt old and decrepit, it seemed that my
lineaments told a different story and he was taken by
them. It had been a long time since anyone had told
me that I was beautiful. Although he continuously
compared my features with my younger years, he
claimed that apart from the colour of my hair I hadn't
changed much. We spoke happily about our past and
favourably of the future but never discussed the reasons
for our being there. As he drove steadily to the
Whistlestop Inn at Talington I began to take stock of him

and noticed that he was far more nervous than he used to be. His demeanour, though still very much a gentleman, had changed slightly. He had lost much of his self-confidence and gave me the impression that his life was no longer important, that he now lived only for those around him. Understandably his life had been tough and it seemed that over the years he had become accustomed to suffering at the hands of his wife's ill–bred son. I was deeply saddened by the stories that he told and constantly wondered what he was still doing there. He and Janice had been together since he and I had separated twenty-five years ago. They had now been married for ten of those years, yet I found it strange that while speaking to him over the phone in all the days that followed he never once claimed that he loved her. It seemed he was grateful but not in love with her, yet he constantly reminded me that he had always loved me.

The Whistlestop Inn was the first pub that I had visited in over thirteen years, so I was surprised that I felt so comfortable there. I had always felt confident with Arch and although I was worried that I might panic once I had stepped outside my comfort zone, I felt more relaxed than I had done in years. He chose an unobtrusive corner of the lounge for us to hide away in and sat down close to me. Clutching the drinks which he had purchased from the bar, we were almost touching and yet so careful not to overstep the mark. At that point neither of us was sure of the other and, just so that we didn't spoil things, we cleverly masked our inner thoughts and feelings with idle banter; within a few hours we had laughed so much it hardly felt like we had been apart. We spoke openly to each other about certain things and even confessed that we had found each other's company even more delightful than we had all those years ago. As we began to unwind, he constantly reminded me of the feelings that he once had for me and repeated the words, 'Marie, why on earth did you leave me?' I couldn't think of any other reason apart from the fact that I was too young. Then I reminded him about Little Molly and my horrific childhood, at which he seemed a little shaken, despite remembering that I had once told him as much as I dared.

The thing I most liked about Arch was that he never pressed me for more information and, although I could see that he was truly saddened by the facts, we both knew that it wasn't the right time to talk about my abusive childhood. As thoughtful as he was, he naturally changed the nature of our conversation to something we were more comfortable with and cheerfully celebrated the reunion that was long overdue.

It was around 2:30pm when we finally left the Whistlestop Inn and as we slowly walked away from the door, I slipped on an icy patch of snow as we laughed on our way to the car. Then I realised that fate had played an ace once again as he put out his hand to stop me from falling. The sudden clasp of our hands felt so natural that neither of us urged to pull away. Instead we gripped each other firmly to secure our grip and sighed with contentment. Desperate to hold onto each other, we did so wholeheartedly while the love we felt transmitted from one to the other. It was at that point that I knew he still cared for me. We giggled at the very thought of falling over but approached his car with caution. He reluctantly let go of my hand and opened the passenger's door, allowing me to climb in. Although it was a bitterly cold day I felt warm and snug as I sat waiting for him to join me; I had never felt so safe. I looked around at the beautiful countryside and the crispness of the newly-fallen snow. It was luminously bright and the sun was shining through the window, warming my face. Had I not known better I could have easily misconstrued that day for a warm summer's day in July.

Five more minutes and our reunion was to come to an end, and already I was beginning to feel sad. But as he climbed into the car next to me, he smiled and warmed my heart. It seemed to take only seconds to arrive back at our original meeting point and for the first time during the whole of that day, I felt really uneasy. We looked across at each other as if our whole world was about to fall apart. I wanted to kiss him but something told me that it wasn't the right time, then suddenly our eyes met and we simply leaned across and kissed so tenderly I felt the emotion run through my veins. He was warm and tender and held on to me with such intensity that he almost made me cry. Having planned our next meeting, he promised me faithfully that he would telephone me. I climbed out of his car knowing that I was going to see him again and yet I could not stop worrying. I knew that I would find it difficult to walk away from him and the very second that I did I was thinking about him. I had never felt so alone. Even though I had been in another relationship for the best part of thirteen years, I felt sad and lonely without him. I had almost reached home when I received an unexpected call from his mobile phone and within split seconds I had convinced myself that he had changed his mind and was phoning to say that he couldn't see me again. But I laughed as he spoke to me through my little pink Samsung. I no longer felt despondent or mournful and instantly felt happy to be alive when he said. 'I am missing you already and can't wait to see you again.' I spontaneously replied, '"Oh my goodness, Arch, I feel the same way too.' I sighed and paused for a moment, 'I thought I had blown it.' 'No, quite the opposite. That one kiss has made me realise what I have been missing. Although there must be something between me and Janice for us to have stayed together for twenty-five years, I have never felt with her the way I felt with you today. And that kiss, well it just threw me. All the feelings that I once had for you came flooding back, so all I know is that now I have found you, I don't ever want to lose you.' I cried into my phone as tears rolled down my cheeks. I just knew from that moment that there were going to be implications, but with anything concerning Arch my heart ruled my head and I was his for the taking. I felt so relieved I could barely speak. Already I knew what each of us was feeling, but still I could not be sure how it was all going to turn out. I had always known Arch to be rational about actions and decisions that he had to make, hence I told him, 'You think too deeply and spoil what should come naturally.' 'And you, my beautiful lady, are very spontaneous and leap before you think!' was his quick reply. Either way I knew both those typical characteristics had their downfalls and could, if we allowed them to, stand in our way of true happiness. We spoke on the phone right up to me reaching my front door. After planning to telephone me the following day, he reluctantly said goodbye. Although I could quite easily have chatted to him for evermore, I said goodbye just as I stepped over the threshold of my home. I no longer felt sad or lonely and, for the first time in twenty-five years, I felt whole again.

As time slowly passed we began to see more of each other and phoned each other most days. It felt the most natural thing in the world to rekindle what we once had and very often he told me, 'If it is at all possible, I think I love you more now than I did back then.' I myself could not possibly have loved him any more than I did. What I had learned was that the love I felt for him was the deepest form of love that any human being could feel. Although he had told me that he felt guilty for deceiving Janice, he also said, 'Everyone deserves a little happiness.' That statement alone told me everything I needed to know. I knew that he wasn't truly happy, that's why he allowed our relationship to go on. In no time at all I was eating out of his hands. I was so in love with him that my long-standing relationship with Peter never really entered my mind. Arch was good for me. He gave me a reason for living and at that particular moment I couldn't see any further forward than the time I spent with him. I thought about what might have been and regularly blamed myself for our relationship not working all those years ago. But during our second meeting when I was alone with him, I let my emotions run totally wild and enjoyed the closeness that I had with him. Feelings that I once perceived as being unnatural now enraptured my soul with sheer ecstasy and total adoration for the man I still loved. It wasn't an ideal situation, I knew that, but because neither of us had planned for anything to happen it appeared so natural. I recall even as a young woman my mind and body had responded well to his touch, although I suffered terrible embarrassment at the thought of enjoying hours of exhaustive intimacy with him. Since I had matured things were different, everything we did together felt perfect. We even agreed that we were perfect soulmates and regularly emphasised the fact that we wanted to spend the rest of our lives together, yet still he had this terrible feeling of guilt whenever he thought of Janice. He often spoke about her and the effort that she had made with his children, but never once did he speak of loving her. Not the way a man should love a woman. He always made it clear that his heart once solely belonged to me and seemed saddened by the fact that he could not just walk away from her. I suppose in a way he was trapped by his own decency. Strangely enough, I respected him for it and loved him all the more for not wanting to hurt her. I just hoped for his sake that she really loved him as much as I did. Already he bore witness to her deceit. Although he tried to clear his mind of it, he had never completely forgotten what had taken place when they had first met. He was such a decent man and, while my heart bled for him, I could not understand his way of thinking. I was totally moved by his consideration for her, but still I could not help wondering if she was really worth it. The years he had spent as a father proved difficult for him and I am sure had it not been for his children, he and Janice would have separated long ago.

I was nurturing a whole lot of troubles and at the age of twenty-five I had never really considered Janice's motive for manipulating him into believing that he wasn't Cheniel's father. I had always assumed that after what had happened during our last encounter, he never had any doubt but it seemed that she was really good at what she did and in a short space of time she had completely turned his notion around. This caused him to lose what little faith he had left in me, which gave her not only the sole freedom to do with his family what she liked, but also the power to finalise what remained of our relationship.

I remember the devastation that I felt when I eventually realised that she had helped to erode all the trust that he ever had in me, and I knew from that moment on it was impossible for me to regain that trust. Never before had I witnessed anything so remorselessly cunning, yet he spoke so highly of her. Although I was mortified at the things she had said to him, my true disappointment lay in Arch. I had invariably thought of him as being strong and impressive, yet suddenly I saw him only as her ally agreeing to support her against all odds. This pitiful man had grown weak; no longer his own being but a shamefully submissive extension of her. Her traits had become his and somehow over the years of humbleness, he had become rather hard-hearted and dispassionate. Although I had always loved him, I found it difficult to understand how he could have allowed that to happen. A situation I would have been infuriated with seemed to have really unnerved him and the long-standing changes now felt natural to him. It's hard for me to imagine what would have been had we stayed together. Would I love him as much as I do now or worship him as naturally as I breathe in air? I would like to think so. It was hard to watch a man that I loved so dearly crumble. If only we could have assessed that when we were together we could have lived in harmony and our lives would not only have been for those whom we cared about but for us to enjoy too, we might have made it.

It breaks my heart to think that in all the years that we have been apart, he has never been truly happy. Instead he overtly informs me that he has lived amongst an oppressive situation which has made him feel depressed and uncomfortable and it is because of that I fail to understand his reasons for staying. When I originally contacted Arch in 2009, I was desperate for him to know how much I still loved him. For years I had been unable to express the way I felt about him, but even after twenty-five years my feelings for him had never changed and for the first time ever I was able to tell him so. I still loved him and, although he had once doubted the fact that I ever loved him at all, I just hoped that after all those years he was able to believe me. But, strange as it seemed, I found myself fighting the same old battle that I had fought all those years ago. No matter how definitively clear I was about my love for him, it seemed that there was always a very important factor that stood in the way of his acceptance of it - the fact that he had always considered Janice as the innocent party in all this, while I considered only his children and our daughter, Cheniel, to fit that role. Although I was never entirely sure when it was that Arch met Janice, I noticed that she gained full control over him and his children almost immediately after I had left. Although I now feel responsible for allowing her to step into my shoes, I must admit that I never envisaged them spending the rest of their lives together. In fact, as she systematically stated that she didn't like children, I never expected their relationship to last, but now I realise that I can only enviously observe the life that she has made with the first man that I ever truly loved.

My life had been nothing like hers, I was certain of that, and pitifully I found myself at times even regretting the survival of my abusive childhood. I got to thinking that it might have been better for all concerned had I not come through it alive. I had never felt proud of myself. Although it seemed at times that my life had favourably influenced others, I wasn't sure if that was enough to compensate for all the ruin I had caused. At that particular time I had never considered myself as being 'one of the lucky ones' who had experienced what some people describe as true contentment, yet during the short time I had spent with Arch and the children I had always felt that because there was love, there was hope.

Monday, 16th March, 2009 things took a turn for the worse. Our lives became more unsettled. Although there wasn't a thought in my head that didn't include Arch, the worry I incurred through our relationship seemed endless. I had always been an intuitive type of person but for some reason I could not work out what it was that he expected of me. I got the impression that he looked on me as being 'safe' yet invulnerable, and at times only seemed to consider Janice's feelings. I had never forgotten that he was always one to surprise me and one day out of the blue he telephoned me and declared, 'What I want most of all is to live with you.' I was so overwhelmed that he left me speechless. Loving and knowing that I was loved had only been something I had previously encountered with our children, but for the first time in my life I knew what I felt about him was right. I loved him deeply and knew only too well that he loved me too, but I knew him better than he thought. He had never been one to follow his own instincts; instead he relied solely on the advice of friends and acquaintances before he would commit himself and faced even more of a dilemma when their advice was not what he wanted to hear. I knew very little about his friends only that most of them were now part and parcel of the marriage vows that he had made to Janice. It seemed that he had allowed her initial friendships to influence him and the relationships that he held with other people, including his own daughter, Nicola, so it was inevitable that the advice those friends offered only benefitted the very few people who had been strong enough to remain within that circle. Of course they only perceived me as an intruder of the marriage, but I considered myself to be more than that. I am the mother of his child. Surely that should account for something.

—ɯɯ—

CHAPTER 20

The Decision to Put Things Right

I had never asked Arch for anything. Even after Cheniel was born, I consciously refused his entry to the maternity ward and returned the beautiful bouquet of flowers that he had brought for me, solely because I did not want to create even more problems for us. In hindsight I now realise that we would have been far better to have faced what problems we had incurred then, sooner than try and sort them out now.

I suppose we were lucky really. From the very first day that we met, we formed this unique level of devotion to each other until it seemed that time and circumstances got in the way. But twenty-five years on it was like that devotion was still intact and our feelings hadn't changed. We spoke openly to each other during the many phone calls that we made, taking a dim view of all the reasons why we had separated, but we knew within our heart of hearts - even with all the regret in the world - we could not change what had happened in the past. He often reminded me that it was water under the bridge; I resented those words. It seemed to me that he had tried to blank the past to help him to cope with the future, but what I really wanted him to do was remember the night that our daughter was conceived. I shall always be proud of her. From the moment she was born she was special. If I had believed back then in fairy tales and enchanted places, I could quite easily have believed that she had been born under a wandering star. Cheniel was a very important part of the triangle and, despite the fact that Janice had previously convinced him otherwise, the decision to put things right was well overdue. I had heard that it was relatively simple to prove paternity, but Janice had such a powerful influence over Arch that she continued to make a simple decision difficult. I despised her for causing so many problems as I realised that, had it not been for her, paternity would have been proven years ago. I had previously kept my opinions to myself so as not to cause any unnecessary problems for him, but at that stage I was considering the right to try and encourage her to dictate less and persuade Arch to make a decision of his own choosing. I had realised that every decision that he had ever made in the past regarding me and Cheniel had been made solely with Janice's welfare at heart, not the future of our daughter. Arch had never been a strong man, so it had proved to be relatively easy for Janice to become the figurehead of his family, and by doing so she had managed to change a whole lifetime of family history. And still she held the key to our future in her hands.

Before I began to write the story of Little Molly, I had no idea I would see Arch again. In the past I had tried so many times to contact him, I had more or less accepted that after twenty-five years he would have dismissed me from his mind or totally forgotten that I ever existed. The memories that I held of him and his two small children had never left me, but in all honesty I had never expected them to remember me. I had always found it difficult to accept that I would never see them again, as I had always hoped that Arch and I would re-unite some day. The fact that my abusive childhood had caused us so many problems was now evidently clear and typically defined my future. It explained the doubts and uncertainties that arose during my life, but still there was no doubt in my mind that Arch was the one that I should have married. I had always loved him but didn't know how to make that clear to him. It was only now the 24th March, 2009 when I could honestly say, 'I truly understand what it was that we had and what it was that I lost.' I had been in contact with him for almost six weeks and could not face the thought of growing old without him. I shamefully admit that I had no respect for his ten-year-old marriage to Janice, as I had never been able to accept that she loved him as much as I did. No matter how much I resented the principle of my own behaviour, I could not respect her moral right to stand in my way again.

That day when my counsellor reminded me that I could not bring back the past, it was a fact that I could not bear to hear. Although his advice had always been good, I thought that I was so in love with Arch that nothing Clive said deterred me from the action I was about to take. I could not reason between right and wrong and the slight possibility of spending the rest of my life with Arch only evoked more of my repressed emotions. I had received counselling for almost five years and assumed because of that I was able to cope with any sudden pressure that life might bring. But following that particular session, I began to wonder about my ability to make important decisions. I thought long and hard about the advice Clive had given me and the way that I felt about Arch, and although I was certain that I wanted to be with him I worried myself senseless about our future and the consequences of still loving him now that he was married. Feeling positively happy when I was with him, I believed that when he returned home to Janice it wasn't because he loved her but more that he was governed by her; it was easier for me to believe that.

I was saddened at the thought of him blaming himself for previous situations that he had experienced at work, which he assumed had caused him the severe bout of depression that he had been nursing for years. Even I knew that it would have taken much more than that to put him in the depressive state that he was in. He wasn't at all like he used to be, he seemed to have lost all his self-confidence and, for reasons unknown to me, he had grown weak and thought himself a far lesser person than anyone else that he knew. It was that which I found hardest to bear. In the past he had always been so sure of himself, fearlessly outspoken and confident through and through. He had worked hard to achieve his goals and, above all else, he had been a terrific father to his children. He was far more worthy of respect than anyone I ever knew and yet my thoughts still swayed from one aspect to another as I constantly wondered about everything he spoke about.

April 6th, 2009 and an early phone call from him caused me to worry. His voice was hoarse and the meaning of his words was unclear. As usual his tiresome relationship with Janice and her son was his main focal point but I listened with the same care and concern as I always had certain that one day he would overcome the long-standing depression which had suppressed him for many years. The words that he muttered were not something that I wanted to hear but I gave him all the time that he needed to open his heart and clear his mind, knowing that at that particular point he needed me. I listened with deep intent, horrified when he told me that, following an argument with Janice, he had spent hours contemplating throwing himself over the edge of the viaduct that dominated the skyline of Monsal Head. It was a place where I had spent many hours playing as a young girl, ignorant of the fact that the magnificent structure had long since become the precarious location that had taken so many lives. The sudden realisation that it had become close to taking the life of the man that I had always loved, suddenly hit home to me. I no longer saw it as my dream castle, my favourite place to run and hide, but the daunting place capable of taunting the many who had already died there.

In the days that followed, I found it difficult to cope with all that was happening. A situation that I had felt so happy about had turned into a complete nightmare.

It seemed that in the past neither of us had proven strong enough to steer away from a life which I now deemed responsible for the deterioration of our minds, so we suffered greatly from the consequences of our unwarranted loyalty. We had reached a situation where it was too late to turn back yet impossible to move forward. The people who we had long since deemed responsible for our wellbeing now clung to us for dear life. Despite pronouncing undeniable love for us, they could not find it in their hearts to set us free.

The 7th April, 2009, and already it had turned 12pm. I felt no shame for having spent yet another morning chatting to him over the telephone. It was all that I looked forward to and yet on that morning I sensed within an instant the apprehension in his voice as he did his utmost to carefully prepare me for a phone call that I was about to receive from Janice. Given his idealistic view of her, he wasn't certain that she was capable of carrying out her fuel-filled threat to confront me, but he declared that he knew her well enough to know that, if she did call to speak to me, it would not be a pleasant experience. Having found out about our meetings, she had spent a considerable amount of time arguing her rights and making demands that he felt that he couldn't keep. It was then that I realised he was fearful of her. Already she had threatened to kill him, seek me out and kill me too, but I wasn't afraid of her. In the past I had suffered greatly at the hands of others, so her morbid threats did not worry me. Having spent a tremendous amount of time trying to calm him down and relieve him of any worry, I reluctantly said goodbye to him and waited anxiously for her to call. As I picked up the phone, I recited the words that I had carefully chosen before she had time to speak. I told her, 'Initially I had no idea you and Arch were still together.' Taking into account all of our history, I was able to engineer a situation that conveniently convinced her that she had nothing to worry about. Although I remained evasive throughout the conversation, I found that I could not lie unnecessarily or intimidate her. Instead I took full responsibility of any wrongdoing and managed to resist any temptation to tell her what I really thought of her. Since I had matured I had become more understanding of people and their feelings. Although I felt that it was only Cheniel who bore the right to grieve any questionable misdemeanour, I couldn't help feeling remorsefully sad for the life that I had allowed to pass me by.

Despite Janice's attempts to carry on the masquerade of pretence that she had so cleverly built around him and his family, for the moral right of everyone concerned I battled through to establish the fact that my daughter Cheniel was also the daughter of Arch Simpson. I had thought long and hard about DNA testing and, although I knew it would change very little for me and Arch, I knew that it could help Cheniel identify an inheritance of beautifully unique characteristics that no-one had the right to take away from her. I had already been made aware that everyone's DNA was unique, unless they had an identical twin of course. But nevertheless I was aware that in all cases our DNA is built half from our mother's DNA and half from our father's, so I knew it was only a paternity test that could bring me peace of mind. However I first had to consider what effect it might have on Cheniel and whether it was the best way forward. And that I could never be sure of. I was nervous. Despite being told by Dr Wilson that testing was simple and painless, I could not help worrying about the psychological effect it might have on her. She had already lived twenty-five years believing that the man I considered to be a very poor substitute was her father and I suppose I was responsible. But I wanted the chance to make amends for that.

I recall the moment she was born. I loved her dearly and thought of her only as my precious little love child, yet for reasons that I was unsure of I was reluctant to inform Arch of her arrival. But his instincts were strong and I supposed for that reason alone he arrived at the hospital only hours after her birth, carrying the most amazing bouquet of flowers. Yet already Nigel dominated my entire life so much that I was afraid to let

Arch see her. It was then that I realised I had made a grave mistake. I felt positively certain that it was too late to put things right and, although I thought I was in love with Arch, I still suffered from the long-term effect of child abuse and couldn't understand what it was exactly that I felt for him. So I continued to punish myself simply because I didn't think I was worthy of him.

It wasn't easy trying to arrange a paternity test; it took time for me to consider what effect it might have on everyone involved and to collect all three samples. Mine was pretty straightforward, but Cheniel had already moved to New Zealand and Janice was doing her best to persuade Arch not to take part at all. Having spent a considerable amount of time discussing it with him, he assured me that he would not allow Janice to dominate the situation as she had done in the past. So no matter what happened, he remained adamant that he would give a sample as promised. Cheniel was the first to respond, after I had sent her two swabs carefully sealed in the DNA collection kit that I had received from a highly skilled forensic team. And on the 6th May, 2009, I received an e-mail from Janice on behalf of Arch. As I read it, her words seemed to jump out at me and rest in the pit of my stomach, 'Send what you have to: Little Ashton, Church Street, Baslow, then whatever the outcome we want nothing more to do with you.' I visualised Arch sitting at the side of her like a nervous little puppy while she eagerly tapped away at their computer keyboard, concocting a message that she no doubt hoped would deliberately intimidate me. But proving that he was Cheniel's father was far too important to me, so I clenched my teeth and counted to ten before preparing what I considered to be the most important kit of all. I got round to posting it on the 8th May, 2009 at 13:07, to arrive no later than the 9th May, 2009 at the address she had specified, but I was worried. I didn't trust her as I knew that she was capable of doing anything to prevent it from happening. She had never shown any compassion, not even towards Cheniel, and it seemed that her main concern was always for herself. She repeatedly told Arch that I posed a threat and tried to convince him that I was only using Cheniel to get what I wanted, but Arch recalled what she had led him to believe all those years ago and which resulted in him losing both me and his daughter. This time he proved to me that he wasn't so gullible.

I was in my early twenties when I gave birth to Cheniel. I believe Janice was older and had been fortunate to have lived a relatively normal life with pretty much everything in its place, whereas I had been damaged, was impaired and lacked so much confidence I had achieved nothing. I was incapable of giving anything but myself. Janice, however, had experienced a good life which made me feel inferior to her, but at the age of 51 I felt as honourable as anyone. I wanted nothing more than the truth to come from this; my daughter was also his daughter and I desperately wanted them to accept that. By the 12th May, 2009, Cheniel, Arch and I had finally completed the DNA test that we had been waiting so long to accomplish. It took very little effort to complete and provide the laboratory with our samples. Once finally submitted, everything else just seemed to fall into place and took only seven days for the forensic team to inform me that the probability of Arch being Cheniel's father was as high as 99,9999%, which left no doubt at all. On the 21st May, 2009 I drew a ring of black ink around the date on my calendar, adding the inscription: 'Received the results of the paternity test.' Glancing over the results, I smiled to myself, proud of the thought that I had been right all along. I had waited twenty-five years for that moment. If I had been wealthy enough to have done it before, things might have been different.

I knew Janice wasn't going to be pleased. It was something that she had purposely prevented us from doing all those years ago, knowing that it was the only thing that would have re-unite us. Arch and I loved each other deeply and she knew that, but it seemed that I was so mixed-up and so afraid of confrontation that I hadn't the will to challenge her.

—m—

CHAPTER 21

A Child's Private Thoughts

Today would have been my father's birthday and as always my mood changed. Saddened at the thought of never seeing him again, I shed a few tears wondering how I had ever managed without him. I began to wonder what he would have thought of all this, certain that I had never told him. I began to shed more tears. As I reached across my desk for a tissue, I caught a glimpse of Cheniel's childhood diary. Her privacy was something that I had never invaded, yet suddenly I felt the urge to prise open the insecure lock that had hidden her most adolescent thoughts for almost thirteen years. Surprised at the lock being broken, I wondered who had taken the liberty of entering her private thoughts without first seeking permission. Angered at the thought, I clenched the pretty pink pocketbook in both hands and nursed it for a while as tears streamed down my face. It was her past but so much truth to confront me with. I cried pitifully as I entered the sad, sad world of the sweetest eleven-year-old girl that anyone could have wished for. 2nd January, 1996 - almost two months before her twelfth birthday - and her diary begins: 'Today I came back from my mum's and when I got back home I ate my dinner then just watched TV until it was time for bed.'

I remember this was a particularly sad time for Cheniel as I had just lost the final battle for custody and was forced by the courts to give up my fight to bring her home. I had been trying to gain custody at that stage for almost seven years; I was tired and hurt so much I had no fight left in me. As I glanced through the record of my little girl's sad and lonely past, I realised that was the year that she had tried to rid herself of the lonely life we had afforded her. On the 3rd January, 1996 she wrote: 'I decided to clean up my bedroom and throw out all the old things and organize the new.' As I flicked through the pages I noticed that there was a certain sadness about her words, something we had instilled into her. Until then I hadn't realised just how sad and lonely she had been. It seemed that she had so little to write about and on the 6th April, 1996, she had made what was going to be her last and final entry. 'Today as Elaine, Dad and I were walking out of our garden gate my brother Ian arrived, he had arranged to sleep over until Tuesday.' She wrote no more until Friday, 13th February, 1998, when I noticed that her style of writing had changed and her words were far more mature; she was soon to be aged fourteen. Her following entry would have made a huge impact on any reader I'm sure: 'I am starting this diary again, I will write my thoughts and feelings and what I have done, please do not read past this point'. She went on to say, 'I have no best friends now, just two good friends: Est and Ali. Mum's in Sri Lanka at the moment, she gets back on Tuesday; I can't wait!' I knew how much she missed me. Although circumstances had forced us to live apart, we yearned to be together and just like her, I too counted every single day that we had to spend apart.

During the short telephone call that I made to her from Sri Lanka, I learned that on Wednesday, 18th February, she and her friend Est had applied for voluntary work. She was all excited and couldn't wait to attend the interview. I hoped with all my heart that she would get that job; she, above everyone, needed to know that she was worthy of something and needed to belong somewhere. Her diary entry for that day explained how she couldn't wait to go to work and how lucky she felt to be able to work. But her last few words read: 'Mum's back tomorrow, I'll phone her as soon as I get in'. The thing that I was most glad about was that she never forgot that I was there for her. I constantly told her that I was only a phone call away, and just like today I would travel across land and sea to be with her. I must admit it feels particularly strange reading through her diary. Although I feel sure that she would not have minded, I took great care not to read anything that I considered too personal. As I continued to idly flick through the pages, I suddenly paused when I noticed that on the 13th April, 1998 she had also made the following entry: 'Today I found out that my biological father is John Arthur Simpson or Arch for short. He has two other children, Adam and Nicola, the last mum had heard they lived at Wingerworth.........I really can't believe it.'

Although I told Cheniel all about Arch when she was just a little girl of 10 years; she could not comprehend the meaning of it all and cleared it from her mind, and because I was merely a novice at parenting I delayed things before I told her again. Unfortunately Nigel lacked empathy and although he was aware of the true facts he made telling her before that time impossible; I regretted ever considering his feelings and wished so many times that I had told her before....it would have been better that way.

There are many more entries in Cheniels diary; however I feel only Cheniel as the right to disclose them if she ever feels the need to write her own autobiography.

—∞—

Epilogue

As a mature woman, I am now old enough to understand that no-one's life is perfect. Everyone has their ups and downs and I, for one, have learned to accept the rough deals with the smooth. I understand more about my parents' lives and how difficult it was for them to care for us as children; after all, looking after ten children could not have been easy.

Although I will never be able to forget what happened to me and my siblings, I no longer despise my parents for it as I realise that in many ways they tried to make amends.

The memories that my children hold of my parents is quite special and I suppose it wouldn't be unfair to say that they made far better grandparents than they did parents, and because of that they earned my children's love and respect. I cannot deny that my own love for my mother never really returned to me until I became an adult, when I found it somewhat difficult to show how much I really cared for her. But despite her past failings, I loved her with all my heart.

My brother, John, is still in self-denial and still blames everyone but himself for the damage that he has caused me. He still finds ways to taunt me and has a tendency to manipulate the foolish into doing what he enjoys doing best... putting fear into innocent people!

—⚬—

Afterword

When I first started writing, it never occurred to me that I would have so much to write about. Although as a child I had always been made aware that I was somewhat different to other children, I never realised just how different until the day I met my counsellor Clive Powell. Once I began to trust and open up to him, it was like unlocking Pandora's Box; there was so much to unleash that I never expected to finish my story and the truth is… I haven't.

In my subsequent book, 'Molly III' (The Untold Story), I continue the sad story of 'Little Molly' the little girl who never experienced a normal childhood but was thrust into a life of sexual abuse and neglect well before she went to primary school.

In 'Molly II' (am I, who I, should be?) I have tried to give the reader some insight to the aftermath that occurred following child abuse. It is a true account of my failed relationships, abduction and attempted murder.

I have written both 'Little Molly' and 'Molly II' (am I, who I, should be?) on memory only.

Visit my website www.littlemolly.co.uk

—m—

Other titles by Rosemarie Smith

Little Molly

Children's books:

Meet the Bubblechomps

Lightning Source UK Ltd.
Milton Keynes UK
UKOW050934031011

179676UK00001B/35/P